IN
CeLeBRaTiON
of the
SeaSONS

IN
CeLeBRaTioN
of the
SeaSoNS

RECIPES FROM A MONASTERY KITCHEN

BROTHER VICTOR-ANTOINE
D'AVILA-LATOURRETTE

LIGUORI/TRIUMPH
LIGUORI, MISSOURI

To Donna and Michael Tighe
Dear and faithful friends in all seasons.

Published by Liguori/Triumph
An Imprint of Liguori Publications
Liguori, Missouri
http://www.liguori.org

Library of Congress Cataloging-in-Publication Data

D'Avila-Latourrette, Brother Victor-Antoine.
     [This good food]
     In celebration of the seasons : recipes from a monastery kitchen / Victor-Antoine
d'Avila-Latourrette.
          p.   cm.
     Originally published: This good food. Woodstock, N.Y.: Overlook Press, c1993.
     Includes index.
     ISBN 0-7648-0571-1
     1. Vegetarian cookery. 2. Cookery, French. I. Title.

TX 837.D27 2000
641.5'636'0944   99–055364

This book is a revised edition of *This Good Food: Contemporary French Vegetarian Recipes from a Monastery Kitchen* published by The Overlook Press, Woodstock, New York.

WINTER

SPRING

SUMMER

AUTUMN

SAUCES, SALSAS, AROMATICS, AND BASICS

INTRODUCTION

This cookbook grew out of requests from friends for a collection of French vegetarian recipes. From then on, I began steadily testing and writing down the recipes that are regularly used here in our monastery, many of which in turn have come from the culinary experiences of monasteries and ordinary homes scattered throughout France. As I continued working with the recipes, I started arranging them in seasonal order, inspiring the format of the book, and emphasizing one of the particular aspects of the monastic cuisine. This book was elaborated in my mind as an organic whole, unified by the theme that all the recipes stemmed from the vegetarian cuisine of France.

The recipes in this cookbook should be examined, tried, and understood in the context of the different aspects that makes this monastic cuisine distinct from other cuisines. There are four essential aspects to the cuisine presented here: seasonal, vegetarian, monastic, and French; and I would like to expand on each of these aspects.

Seasonal "It is a question of being in harmony with nature's cycles, of looking to the seasons to find a healthy cuisine," says Chef Georges Blanc. The monastic fare is basically seasonal. First of all, the monk's life itself is ordered and deeply affected by the rhythm of the seasons. His daily schedule, work, worship, and so on, all change according to the cycle of the seasons. Monks

themselves usually grow and raise their own food for the monastic table. This means we are able to eat our own fresh fruits and vegetables when they are in season and store the rest for consumption during the winter months. Our gardens, our orchards, and our farm animals provide us with our daily fresh basic food (vegetables, fruits, eggs, milk, butter, cheese, yogurt, and so on), which is complemented by staples bought at the local markets (grains, beans, rice, pasta, coffee, tea, for example).

In the introductory presentation to each season and the corresponding recipes, I try to put in context and share with the reader how the rhythm of the seasons shapes the daily life of the monk; and how, ultimately, his life becomes integrated by the harmonious interaction with, and assimilation of, the cycles of nature, the cycle of the liturgy, the cycles of the heart and those of life itself.

For any cook, two advantages of trying to keep a seasonal cuisine are the facts that fruits and vegetables are at their best when eaten fresh; and second, but equally important, their cost is reduced considerably when in season. This does not mean that the recipes presented here should be used *only* during the assigned season. I encourage the reader to try them especially during that particular season, even more so, if you happen to live in the Northeastern part of the United States—particularly the Hudson Valley—as I do, but by no means feel confined or limited by this arrangement. Feel free, if you wish, to experiment with these recipes at any time in or out of season. Let us not forget that the seasons themselves interlap. Certainly, what is appropriate for late autumn may also be appropriate for winter itself, and the same can be said for early spring.

Vegetarian Vegetables play an important role in monastic cooking

and in the eating habits of monks. The monastic diet has been essentially vegetarian throughout the centuries, especially for those who live under the rule of Saint Benedict, as we do in this small monastery. Dairy products and seafood are allowed in the monastic diet and consequently are included in this collection.

In France, a country with a deep and rich agricultural tradition, there is a renewed interest in vegetables and vegetarianism in general. So much so that the well-known French gastronome, Christian Millau, calls it "the triumph of the vegetables."

Vegetables have always been intrinsic to French cooking, but lately and increasingly, we see an emphasis on them which is most apparent in their beautiful and imaginative presentation in vegetarian and nonvegetarian cooking. The recipes in this book, faithful to their monastic inspiration, deliberately exclude meat dishes. As an alternative, the cuisine presented here exalts health, nutrition, and most certainly good taste *à la française*. A vegetarian meal, when well prepared and attractively presented in courses, following the elegant pattern of a traditional French meal, can become a true reason for celebration.

Monastic

Monastic The character of monastic cookery is usually known for its simplicity, sobriety, wholesomeness, and basic good taste. Individuals who have partaken of the hospitality of monasteries in France often remark about the balanced and healthy diet of monks, which usually consists of products from the monastery farm and gardens, prepared and presented with simplicity and good taste.

Monastic cooking is something more than just plain ordinary good food. Though marked by certain frugality and simplicity, monastic cooking relies a great deal on the freshness of the products to assure its quality of excellence. It also counts on the wisdom of local tradition, handed down from generation to generation, and the resourcefulness of the cook's imagination for creating thrifty, delicious, sensible, and well-balanced meals. The simple monastic cuisine does not lack elegance, for simplicity itself is synonymous with elegance. Monastery kitchens are usually arranged with a great deal of efficiency and industry, so as to promote, with loving care, the health and well-being of the monks by creating foods of outstanding quality.

French

French People from all around the world travel to France to enjoy and savor the quality of French food. In this book, the entire gamut of recipes come from France. They come from monasteries and ordinary French homes. A few recipes, and they are easily recognizable, might have had their origins in neighboring countries, such as Spain or Italy, but after undergoing some adaptation, they have become, by assimilation, part of the French repertoire. This collection of recipes does not pretend to represent the gastronomical world of the *haute cuisine francaise*. Instead they reflect more the family and country style of French cooking, the daily, earthy, honest, basic food which forms the daily fare of monasteries. Many of the recipes are old family recipes with which I was brought up, others come from different monastic backgrounds, and quite a few others from friends scattered throughout all the corners of our beloved land of France.

French cooking today, especially French vegetarian cooking, is constantly evolving, as we see, for example, in the exquisite cuisine of the prominent young chef Guy Savoy, who has developed a passion for vegetables to the extent of creating something magical, something sublime with them. French vegetarian cooking, though based in the traditional French cuisine, is emerging these days with some very subtle nuances and with obvious splendid results. New techniques and methods of preparing vegetables are experimented with, new seasonings are tried, ultimately creating a cuisine that exalts fine taste. In French kitchens, today as in the past, vegetables, grains, herbs, and fruits are treated with the respect and attention they obviously deserve. All the most recent cooking techniques in France are directed to enhance the quality and the texture, the flavor and the color, of each individual vegetable. The end result is exquisite to both the eyes and the palate.

Finally, before I put an end to this introduction, I wish to encourage all the readers of this book to experiment with these recipes with joy and without fear. Don't be afraid to change certain methods or improve on them, if you wish to do so.

Please refer to the back of the book for some of the basic sauces, vinaigrettes, pastry dough, and so on, required in some of the recipes in this book.

Enjoy *la bonne table* and, of course, this particular form of vegetarian cooking. *Bon appétit*!

BROTHER VICTOR-ANTOINE
SEPTEMBER 8, 1999
FEAST OF THE NATIVITY OF THE MOTHER OF GOD

SOME NOTES ABOUT MONASTIC LIFE

Thus there were in the desert monasteries which were so many temples filled
with heavenly choirs of men who spent their lives singing the Psalms, reading
the sacred Scriptures, fasting, praying, seeking their consolation in the hope of
joys to come, working with their hands in order to give alms, living all together
in perfect charity and a union worthy of admiration; thus one could see in
these places as it were an altogether different country cut off from the rest of
the world, and the fortunate inhabitants of that country had no other thought
than to live in love and justice.

SAINT ATHANASIUS' LIFE OF SAINT ANTONY OF THE DESERT,
WRITTEN IN THE THIRD CENTURY

Saint Athanasius thus describes the life led by the early monks in the deserts
of Egypt. The origins of the monastic life go back to the Gospels—to the
teachings and example of Jesus himself, and to the prophetic figure of John
the Baptist, whose voice cried out in the desert: "Prepare the way of the Lord." The
monastic ideal took root in the early years of Christianity, and it has always re-
mained an integral part of the life of the Church. From the very beginning, there
were Christians who took to heart Christ's invitation to leave all they possessed to
follow him. Obviously, the times have changed since Christ first uttered his invita-

tion of total renunciation to those who can accept it. Nevertheless, throughout the passing of the centuries, there have always been those who, upon hearing the call and recognizing his voice in the depths of their hearts, have felt irresistibly compelled to leave everything behind to follow the Lord.

From the time of Saint Antony on, many have felt the call to that mysterious place called desert. It was the "waste land," always the symbol and reality of total renunciation, where one went to do battle with the forces of evil and to seek God alone with purity of heart. For all monks, those following either the cenobitic or the eremitical life, the desert ideal remains the prototype of what their monastic life is meant to be: a generous renunciation of evil and all that is not God; a dying to selfishness so that the true self may emerge; a burning desire and an unquenchable thirst for the living God and lastly, a striving for total fidelity to the smallest commandments of the Gospel so that their lives may be transformed by the power of God's love and transfigured into the likeness of him.

Very often, monastic life is not understood by society or even by fellow Christians. The emphasis on renunciation, on seclusion, on absolute dedication to prayer, makes people think it is a very negative way of life. Some think of monks as being odd people, flying away from the company of their fellow human beings and the responsibilities of the world for some mysterious reason. However, monks and those who have come from time to time to share their life know this is not true. Prayer opens their hearts totally to God and to their fellowman. If they follow the path of self-renunciation, it is simply because Christ demands it of those whom he calls. If they retire into the desert to pray continuously, they take in their hearts the concerns of all humankind. Prayer expands the dimensions of the heart, making it vast and capable of containing both God and all his people. Prayer, when perfected by grace, leads the monk to recognize the presence of Christ in every human being.

Like the Church, Christian monasticism was born in the East. This is an important fact to keep in mind when we try to understand it and see its continuity to our times. Saint Benedict was a monk in the fifth century, born near Rome and educated there. Having received the Eastern monastic tradition from Saint Antony, Pachomius, Basil, John Cassian, and also from those who preceded him in the

West, he wrote down his "little rule for beginners" as he called it, which has been followed since by countless men and women. Like the earlier Fathers, Saint Benedict conceived the monastic life as a way of seeking God by means of conversion and true repentance, purity of heart, continual prayer, sacred reading, silence, stability, obedience, manual work, and hospitality. All this lived in the enclosure of the monastery "under a Rule and an Abbot."

For Saint Benedict, the monk has to sincerely engage himself in the life-task work of conversion and humble repentance. In the Rule, on the Chapter on Prayer, Saint Benedict counsels the monk to pray with repentance and tears of compunction. The monk, as he becomes more and more aware of his own sinfulness and that of others, cries out day and night from the depths of his heart; "Lord have mercy on me, a sinner." The monk's striving for unceasing prayer is mainly expressed by the celebration of the *Opus Dei*, the hours of silent prayer, the practice of *lectio divina*, and by the continual efforts to remain conscious of the living God, in whose presence the monk stands.

Prayer, in the eyes of Saint Benedict, best expresses the totality of the monk's involvement with God. It is therefore natural that the monk's life should gravitate towards prayer, towards living in close communion with God. In order to help him do this more effectively, Saint Benedict provides the monk with another important means: the practice of *lectio divina*, which is the assiduous studying and reading of sacred Scripture, so that, little by little, the Word of God will penetrate more and more to the innermost place in a monk's heart and thus become his daily bread.

The monk, when not occupied with formal prayer and sacred reading, is meant to be occupied with manual work. "They are truly monks," says Saint Benedict, "when they live by the labor of their hands as did our Fathers and the Apostles." For monks, humble manual labor is part of the universal precept given by God to sinful man (Gen 3:19). The balance between prayer, sacred reading, and manual work—which includes work in the garden and tending the animals—constitutes the life-rhythm of the monastic day.

Another important element of monasticism is the reception of guests. Saint Benedict prescribes in Chapter 53 of the Rule that "all guests that come to the monastery should be welcome as Christ; for He himself will say 'I was a guest, and you took me in'" (Mt 25:35). This should not surprise us, for Saint Benedict took the Gospel literally and as such he taught it to his disciples. We read in the prologue of the Rule: "Let us encompass ourselves with faith and the practice of good works, and guided by the Gospel, tread the path he has cleared for us. Thus may we deserve to see him, who has called us into his Kingdom."

Finally, Saint Benedict sees the monastery as "a school in the Lord's service" where the monk comes to be formed, and the monastic community as a real, stable family centered around the Abbot, the Father of the community. Saint Benedict envisions in the community the harmony of an ideal family where the brethren mutually support each other, and where the Father leads them wisely and prudently in their quest for God. The Abbot, for Saint Benedict, is much more than just the juridical figure that the Superior is in other religious communities. In fact, there is no parallel. For Saint Benedict, the Abbot is a Father who "takes the place of Christ" in the community and around whom are built the stable fraternal relationships of the monastic family. The Abbot, by his example and teaching, encourages the monks to love one another as brothers, practicing charity in forbearance, patience, and mutual respect. It is in the light of Saint Benedict's conception of the monastic community as a family that we must understand the vow of stability. It is because the monk is part of a permanent concrete family that he vows stability to a particular monastery. By the vow of stability, the monk is bound to remain until death at the monastery of his profession. This helps the monk to surrender "mobility," one of the physical expressions of pride, independence, and self-will, to the healing yoke of obedience. Stability to a particular monastic family brings to the heart of a monk the gift of security and inner peace.

BROTHER VICTOR-ANTOINE
OUR LADY OF THE RESURRECTION MONASTERY
LA GRANGEVILLE, NEW YORK

How To Use
This Cookbook

Daily cooking, either in the monastery, the family, for couples without children, or for persons living alone, is a challenge. Most cooks aim at preparing good, balanced, appetizing meals every day, but this is not always easy. At times we find such obstacles as the lack of sufficient time for a worthy preparation. Other times, after a hectic day we are simply too tired. For many, there is also the consideration of the cost for food. Obviously, we must make a distinction about the everyday cuisine and the cuisine for special occasions and celebrations, as when we entertain friends.

Ideally the everyday cuisine should meet the following criteria: it should be balanced, tasty, simple, easy, quick, economical, and, as much as possible, make use of fresh ingredients.

The festive cuisine for special occasions may also follow most of the criteria of the everyday cuisine, but instead of being easy, quick, and economical, one may try dishes that are a bit more complex, require longer preparation, and, perhaps but not always, may be more expensive. In order to follow these criteria as closely as possible, I think it helps a great deal and saves a lot of time if we get used to planning the menu for the week.

To help the reader see how one can plan a balanced vegetarian menu by making use of the recipes in this book, I present here as a loose "model" two sets of recipes for each season. The first may be used as an example of the everyday cuisine and the second for that of festive or special occasions. These menus follow the pattern of an ordinary French meal: soup, main course, salad, cheese, and dessert.

Winter

Daily Meal

Potato and Leek Soup

Rice Bread

Bean Sprouts Salad

Cheese or Yogurt

Apple Flan Alsatian Style or Fruit

Sunday Meal

Potage of Brussels Sprouts

Leek Tart

Fennel With Lemon

Salad Saint Mary Magdalene

Floating Island

Christmas Meal

Artichokes Gasconne Style

Mushroom Soufflé

Mixed Salad

Floating Island

Lenten Meal

Tomato-Lentil Soup

Saint Joseph's Salad

Old-Fashioned Bread Pudding

Spring

Daily Meal

Rice Soup

Sorrel Omelet

Parsley Potatoes

Red Salad

Cheese or Yogurt

Apple Tart or Fresh Fruits

Sunday Meal

Endive Soup From the Ardennes

Crêpes With Spinach Filling

Saint Joseph's Salad

Cheese

Lemon Soufflé

Easter Meal

Cream of Sorrel Soup

Scallops in Breadcrumbs

Asparagus With Garlic Sauce

Spinach Salad

Apple Tart

Pentecost

Avocado Mousse

Saint Daniel's Fettuccine

Salad of the Islands

Chocolate Mousse

Summer

Daily Meal

    Lemony Carrot Soup

    Simple Piperade

    Surprise Salad

    Cheese or Yogurt

    Melon With Strawberries

Sunday Meal

    Creamy Chervil Soup

    Stuffed Tomatoes Provençal Style

    Salad of the Islands

    Cheese

    Clafoutis

Saint Benedict's Feast Day Meal (July 11)

    Beets Provençal Style

    Couscous With Mediterranean Sauce

    Surprise Salad

    Oranges for Saint Benedict's Day

Assumption Day (August 15)

    Iced Tomato Soup

    White Tuna and Potatoes

    Spinach Salad

    Peach Mousse

Autumn

Daily Meal

    Harvest Bean Soup

    Fillet of Sole Alsatian Style

    Spanish Salad

    Cheese or Yogurt

    Pumpkin and Apple Compote

Advent Meal

    Healthy Bouillon

    Omelette With Peppers

    Carrot Salad Bonaparte

    Light Waffles

Sunday Meal

    Saint Geneviève's Soup

    Lentil Moussaka

    Green String Beans Spanish Style

    Saint Martin's Salad

    Cheese

    Saint Sabas' Raspberries With Cream

WiNTeR

He that will not labor in harvest,
must begge in winter.

ENGLISH PROVERB, SIXTEENTH CENTURY

There is no unbelief;
Whoever plants a seed beneath the sod
And waits to see it push away the clod,
He trusts in God.
Whoever says when clouds are in the sky,
Be patient, heart, light breaketh by and by,
Trust the Most High.

Whoever sees 'neath the field of winter snow,
the silent harvest for the future grow,
God's power must know.

EDWARD BULWER-LYTTON

Open wide the window of our spirits,
O Lord, and fill us full of light:
open wide the door of our hearts,
that we may receive and entertain you
with all our powers of adoration and love.

CHRISTINA ROSSETTI

With the arrival of winter, all garden work practically ends here in our small monastery. A few weeks earlier, the last bulbs were set in the ground and the last of the vegetables harvested—carrots, beets, turnips, leeks, chard, Brussels sprouts. These and other vegetables picked in the fall—potatoes, squash, onions, and so on—will carry us through the winter. There are marvelous hearty soups that one can create with these winter vegetables. And whenever we make soup here, we make it to last for days. During the winter, one never tires of soups. When the garden is finally put to rest for the winter, some mulching is done around the flower gardens to protect the perennials that will return in spring. Then, the tools are cleaned and stored for the season, and the only garden-related activity that remains even during the coldest of days is that of building up the compost pile for next year's gardens. And, of course, wood-splitting, carrying the logs indoors, and tending the stoves just begins. But all of this, with the daily care of our animals, is a pleasant change from the intense involvement with the gardens during the growing seasons.

During the somber and cold days of winter here along the border between eastern New York and New England, the beauty and the quality of the light are particularly striking. The fiery intensity of summer changes to become a luminous autumnal glow; now, in winter, as the light recedes, soft pale colors turn gradually to gray as dusk overtakes the countryside. At other times of the year, many of us may take light for granted, but this is not so during the winter season. If anything, winter, because of its shorter days and longer nights, makes us more intensely aware of our own deep instinctual need for light. The early days of winter, with their longer and darker nights, coincide in our hemisphere with the Christian season of Advent. And Advent is a time of waiting for the Light which will shine at Christmas.

As we approach Christmas, the days grow shorter, the air grows colder, and a quiet stillness settles at large on the physical world. All living things that must survive the winter out-of-doors draw deep into themselves. The trees retract their sap, the animals in the forest hibernate, the living creatures that continue to move around in the cold, snow-covered world, take care to conceal where their food stores are.

For the household it is also a time of turning inward; of wood-splitting and preparations for keeping warm through the cold months ahead; of cozy friendly gatherings around the fire; of warm family evenings in the kitchen; of quiet time for reading and listening to music; of planning for gifts that will be made or bought; and of preparing food supplies that will be needed for Christmas baking. Most important of all for many people is the inner preparation for the yearly celebration of Christmas, the solemn commemoration of the birth of Christ.

In the monastery as in the home, the Advent wreath, made of fresh evergreens, is a symbol of this time of hope and waiting. The greens used in the wreath are of the color always considered from antiquity on as representing hope; and the wreath itself, inherited from a pre-Christian Germanic custom of making a wheel of fire at the winter solstice, has come to represent a legendary cycle of thousands of years from Adam to Christ, a waiting period for the deliverance of humankind. Advent then is about coming, and about waiting for the coming. It is a very special season of hope that links the coming of the promised Messiah in Jesus with the coming of Christ into our own hearts after a period of preparation, and the coming of Christ again in the Parousia, that is, at the end of time. Like other seasons of the liturgical year, Advent commemorates something of the past in order to heighten our awareness of the same mystery at work now, today, in our own lives, and to give direction for the still awaited future.

Early on, at the very threshold of the Advent season, the feast of Saint Nicholas is celebrated on December 6. As a young orphan, Nicholas distributed all his wealth to the poor and consecrated himself to God. He was made Bishop of Myra and died around 342. He is credited with setting free captives and with saving schoolboys from death and young girls from dishonor. Saint Nicholas is particularly honored in Greece, Italy, and Russia, and also in the Netherlands and other Germanic countries, where his was known as "Santa Klaus." In many of these northern European countries, presents are exchanged on his feast day. From Europe, the lovely custom of giving gifts during the Christmas season came to America. Because his feast usually falls within the first week of Advent, he is considered an Advent saint who points joyfully toward the coming of the Lord. His feast is celebrated in some European monasteries with revivals of medieval plays about his life.

All the Advent preparations find fulfillment on Christmas and the twelve days that follow. Everywhere there is a sense of joyful expectancy as families sit down to Christmas Eve supper—the Réveillon de Noël in France, the Nochebuena of Spain and Spanish-speaking countries, the Notte di Natale in Italy. The Christmas Eve gatherings in this country and all around the world are part of the precious memories that both children and adults alike carry with them *all* their lives. Since reverence and joy belong together, the old European custom of dancing around the lighted tree and the singing of Christmas carols makes a beautiful culmination for the family gathering on this holy night. Many families then proceed to attend the traditional Christmas Midnight Mass or other religious services on Christmas morning. On Christmas morning itself, the hushed reverence of the night before turns to full jubilation.

And while the Christian community is busy celebrating its splendid festival, the Jewish community also rejoices during these days of the winter solstice by celebrating Hanukkah, the Jewish Festival of Lights. Hanukkah commemorates the victory of the Maccabees over the invading army of Syrians, and a miracle of lights associated with this victory. To commemorate this miracle, Jews around the world light Hanukkah candles for eight days, exchange gifts, and eat special foods, such as potato pancakes.

After Hanukkah and Christmas, the most important holiday of the season is New Year's Day. January is usually one of the coldest months of the year or, as someone once put it, "the blackest month of the year," and while the winter's inhospitable weather may render many outdoor activities less desirable, it provides the special opportunity for intimate gathering of friends, especially on New Year's Day, around the fire. There, in the warmth of the fireplace, lovely home-baked food is offered to friends to help take away the chill of winter. One of the charms of an otherwise dreary winter is that it seems to bring families and friends together in a unique way by allowing them to share a closeness not always possible during the warmer months.

From the Christmas jubilation and the cozy celebrations of the New Year, we complete the Christmas cycle on the twelfth day, January 6, the feast of the Epiphany. Western Christians tend to place the emphasis of the Epiphany feast on the visit of the Magi to the newly born Messiah; the Eastern Christians, however, emphasize on this day the baptism of Christ in the Jordan River and the first manifestation of the Mystery of the Trinity therein.

Whichever aspects of the Epiphany we may choose to emphasize, we never escape from the harsh reality of being in the winter. T. S. Eliot reminds us of this in his beautiful poem, "The Journey of the Magi"

> *A cold coming we had of it,*
> *Just the worst time of the year*
> *For a journey, and such a long journey:*
> *The ways deep and the weather sharp,*
> *The very dead of winter.*

After Epiphany, the rest of January seems buried in deep cold frosty silence. The wintry weather seems to chill us to our very marrow. The monastic solitude is complete, cherished, and more real than ever; the harsh-savage beauty of winter inspires prayer and contemplation. Just when one is beginning to feel at home in our snowbound winter solitude, February, the shortest month of the year, arrives. February begins with the beautiful feast of Candlemas on the second day of the month. It is the fortieth day after Christmas, and it is a special day in the Catholic tradition, commemorating the presentation by the Virgin Mother of her Child in the Temple, and her making an offering to the Lord in accord with Jewish custom. On this day, candles are blessed and then used in the procession that leads to the celebration of Mass. Candles are, in general, very expressive of the devotional life of monasteries and families: there are the four candles in the Advent wreath, lit on successive weeks before Christmas; the paschal candle lit at Easter—and *all* have a special meaning. Candles are used in many human celebrations across all cultures, especially in worship and family celebrations, and in time of quietness and reflection. The dancing yet steady flame of a candle teaches us about the seen and the unseen in ways more eloquent than words. It helps create an atmosphere of intimacy, and it helps focus family togetherness, since candlelight speaks to old and young alike. Candles brighten our dark winter nights. Candles speak of intangible realities. Candles are God's messengers.

SOUPS AND
APPETIZERS

HEALTHY BOUILLON
BOUILLON DE SANTÉ

6-8 servings

8 cups water
2 large onions, sliced
2 large carrots, sliced
1 celery stalk, sliced
minced parsley and thyme to taste
4 garlic cloves, minced
1 bay leaf
salt and pepper to taste
1 bottle (4 cups) dry white wine

1. Pour the water into a large soup pot, add the sliced vegetables, herbs, salt, and pepper; bring to a boil. Let it boil for about 15 minutes over medium heat; simmer over low-medium heat for 30 minutes.

2. Add the wine and bring to a boil again; reduce heat to medium and cook for 10 to 15 minutes. Remove from heat and let sit for a few minutes. Just before serving, pass the bouillon through a fine strainer. This soup can be served hot or refrigerated and served cold. Remove bay leaf.

Bouillon is probably the most popular drink in France, since one learns to drink it from early infancy. Both children and the elderly, to say nothing of the sick, drink bouillon as a medicine and as something fortifying to help regain one's strength. It is particularly appropriate when one has stomach problems or when one is recuperating from a cold. This recipe can be served hot in the winter or chilled for a few hours and served cold during the hot weather months.

Peasant Soup
Potage Paysan

6-8 servings

2 carrots, peeled
2 white turnips
2 leeks (or 2 onions), diced
12 cups water
1 cup lentils
1 cup rice
4 garlic cloves, minced
1 bay leaf
1/4 lb okra, chopped (optional)
2 vegetable bouillon cubes (optional)
salt and pepper to taste
2 Tbsps olive oil or butter
fresh parsley, minced

1. Finely slice and dice all the vegetables. In a large soup pot or casserole, pour in the water and add all the ingredients. Boil for 10 minutes, then reduce heat to medium.

2. Cook the soup over a medium heat for about 1 hour, stirring from time to time, and adding more water if needed.

3. Add salt and pepper, and any of the optional ingredients mentioned above. Simmer for about 10 minutes. Just before serving add 2 tablespoons of olive oil or butter, sprinkle with minced parsley, and serve while it is hot.

This is a very simple and wholly nutritious soup, and like most peasant and homey soups in France, one can make use of all the fresh vegetables available during the season.

POTATO AND LEEK SOUP
SOUPE AUX POMMES DE TERRE ET POIREAUX

6 servings

5 Tbsps butter
8 cups water
6 leeks (white part only)
6 large potatoes, peeled and diced
salt and pepper to taste
chervil or parsley, finely chopped

1. Melt the butter in a large soup pot and throw into it the well-washed leeks cut in small round slices. Sauté them for 2 or 3 minutes, then add the water and potatoes. Cook the soup over a medium heat for about 1 hour.

2. When the soup is done, add salt and pepper according to taste, mash the potatoes a bit inside the soup and stir the soup very well. As you serve each bowl, sprinkle a bit of well-minced chervil on the top, or parsley if you happen to be out of chervil.

A very basic and simple soup for wintertime. If you wish to add some fanciness to it, pour one tablespoon heavy cream into each serving dish. Serve piping hot with small slices of toasted French bread.

Many soups that evolved through the centuries in the French provinces are based more on vegetables than on meats or even meat stocks, and are frankly described as "healthy": potages de santé. Their recipes are ancient, as basic as the need for cabin-bound men to go out with their livestock in the first days of spring and gather the grasses and roots of the awakening meadows. These soups depend on spinach and sorrel, and all the herbs, and mushrooms, and fresh milk and cream and butter, all tasting perennially and incredibly delicious after the long dark months of eating stored roots like turnips, and potatoes, and cabbages and onions and garlic.

M. F. K. FISHER
THE COOKING OF PROVINCIAL FRANCE

TOMATO/GARLIC SOUP
SOUPE DE TOMATES À L'AIL

4-6 servings

14 cloves of garlic, well minced
1/2 cup olive oil
6 cups water
2 vegetable bouillon cubes
12 ozs tomato sauce
8 slices French bread, diced
1 bay leaf
salt and pepper to taste
2 eggs, well beaten
pinch of cayenne pepper

1. In a soup pot, sauté garlic in olive oil over low heat without allowing it to brown or burn. Stir continuously. Add 3 cups water, the bouillon cubes, and the tomato sauce. Stir well.

2. Add remaining water, the French bread, bay leaf, salt, and pepper. Bring to a boil, stirring continually, then reduce heat and let cook for about 15 minutes. Simmer slowly for another 15 minutes.

3. In a deep bowl, beat the 2 eggs gently, adding half a cup of the soup and blending the mixture very well. Pour this mixture slowly into the soup, stirring constantly. Simmer for another 2 minutes. Remove bay leaf and serve hot.

his is a very popular dish in Spain and southern France, where one can find as many variations of this basic soup as there are households. A piping hot garlic soup is particularly appetizing on a cold winter day.

WHITE BEAN SOUP SAINT SCHOLASTICA
SOUPE SAINTE SCHOLASTIQUE

4 servings

3 qts water
6 Tbsps brown lentils
6 Tbsps dried split peas
4 Tbsps white beans or lima beans
1 onion, finely cut
2 large carrots, finely cut
2 medium-sized turnips, finely cut
1 celery stalk, finely cut
1 small lettuce head, minced
4 Tbsps butter
salt and pepper to taste

1. Pour water into a large soup pot. Add the lentils, spilt peas, and beans; bring the water to a boil.

2. Add the onion, carrots, turnips, and celery stalk. Continue boiling over medium heat for about 30 minutes. Then add the lettuce. Let it simmer for another 30 minutes over very low heat.

3. When the soup is done, add the butter, salt, and pepper, stir well; let it simmer for about 10 minutes. Serve hot garnished with croutons.

he feast of Saint Scholastica is celebrated on February 10. It is one of those lovely monastic feasts that brighten our long dark winters. She was the twin sister of Saint Benedict and a close collaborator in his work. Once a year she was permitted to see her brother, who used to come part of the way to meet her outside the monastery walls. As Saint Benedict is considered the father of the monks in the West, so is his sister Scholastica rightfully considered and esteemed as the beloved mother of nuns.

POTAGE OF BRUSSELS SPROUTS
POTAGE AUX CHOUX DE BRUXELLES

6–8 servings

4 Tbsps butter
1 lb Brussels sprouts, sliced in fourths
1 lb potatoes, diced
3 leeks or onions, sliced
2 garlic cloves, minced
8 cups water
1 bay leaf
pinch of dried thyme
salt and pepper to taste
2 cups milk
freshly grated Parmesan cheese

1. Boil separately 8 Brussels sprouts sliced in four even quarters to be served on the top of the soup as garnish.

2. Melt the butter in a saucepan and sauté the Brussels sprouts, potatoes, leeks or onions, and garlic for a minute or two. Stir continually. Add the water and spices and cook slowly over low-medium heat until the soup is done. It takes about 40 to 45 minutes to cook the soup thoroughly. Remove the bay leaf.

3. When the soup is done, add the milk and stir well. Put the soup in a blender on a high speed until thoroughly blended and serve hot. Serve the soup in individual bowls and garnish each with the Brussels sprouts that were boiled separately. Sprinkle with grated Parmesan cheese.

Beautiful soup, so rich and green,
Waiting in a hot tureen!
Who for such dainties would not stoop?
Soup of the evening, beautiful Soup!

LEWIS CARROLL
ALICE IN WONDERLAND

Saint Valentine Soup
SOUPE SAINT VALENTIN

4 servings

2 carrots
3 leeks (or two medium-sized onions)
2 stalks celery
1 green bell pepper
8 cups water
10 Tbsps dried split peas
8 Tbsps vegetable oil
salt and pepper to taste

1. Slice the carrots, leeks, celery, and pepper, and chop them into small pieces.

2. Pour the water into a large casserole or soup pot and add all the vegetables. Bring to a boil and then cook slowly over a low flame for about 1 hour. Add the remaining ingredients and more water if necessary. Stir well and continue cooking for another 15 minutes. Simmer for another 10 to 15 minutes and serve the soup very hot.

 his is an excellent soup for the long winter nights, and especially on Saint Valentine's day!

Long is our Winter,
Dark is our night,
Come set us free,
O Saving Light!

FIFTEENTH CENTURY HYMN

TAPENADE
TAPENADE

6-8 servings

8 ozs pitted black olives (about 20 or more olives)
4 ozs anchovies with oil
1/3 cup capers
1/2 cup olive oil
juice of 1 lemon
2 garlic cloves, minced
1 Tbsp Dijon mustard
1 dried bay leaf
pinch of dried thyme

1. Finely chop the olives, anchovies, and capers. Place them in a blender, add the olive oil and lemon juice; blend until the mixture is thoroughly smooth.

2. Add the rest of the ingredients and more olive oil if necessary and continue to blend until the mixture has the consistency of smooth dark butter. Spread over slices of French bread or crackers and serve as appetizers.

This concoction is quintessentially Mediterranean and above all Provençal. It denotes the aroma and the taste that one associates with the sunny rich land of Provençe. Tapenade can be served in multiple ways; as a filling for hard-boiled eggs, tomatoes, or avocados, as well as a spread for any sort of bread or crackers. The true Provençal loves to spread it on fresh *pain de campagne*. One could substitute any fresh-baked bread.

ARANCINI
ROQUETTES AUX RIS

10 croquettes

1 lb arborio rice
salt to taste
1 egg, beaten
1 egg yolk, beaten
2 ozs Parmesan cheese, grated
white pepper to taste
flour, as needed
2 eggs, lightly beaten
breadcrumbs, as needed
olive oil, as needed

1. Boil the rice in salty water until done. Taste and see that the rice is properly cooked. Drain and allow it to cool.

2. Place the rice in a deep bowl. Add the beaten egg, egg yolk, grated cheese, and white pepper. Mix well all ingredients. Let the mixture stand for about 30 minutes. It can also be refrigerated.

3. Lightly wet your hands and gently roll the croquettes into 10 even balls. When the croquettes are well formed, roll each one first into the flour, then the beaten eggs, and last into the breadcrumbs. Refrigerate for 1 hour.

4. Pour olive oil into a skillet and raise the heat to medium-high. Fry the croquettes two at a time. Make sure they are fried on all sides. Remove them and place on paper towels to absorb the oil. Keep them in a 200° F oven until ready to serve. They make excellent appetizers.

MAIN DISHES

Eggs With Mushrooms in Ramekins
Oeufs en Cocotte à la Bergère

6 servings

4 Tbsps butter
3 lbs mushrooms, sliced
1 medium-sized onion, chopped
freshly grated nutmeg
2 Tbsps finely minced fresh parsley
6 eggs
salt and freshly ground pepper to taste

1. Melt 2 tablespoons butter in a skillet and sauté the mushrooms and onions for about 4 to 5 minutes over low to medium heat. When the mushrooms are cooked, add the nutmeg and finely minced parsley and blend thoroughly.

2. Butter well the inside of 6 small porcelain bowls and fill them with the mushrooms, creating a nest in the center. Break an egg in the center of each nest. Sprinkle salt and pepper on the top of each.

3. Place the bowls in a large saucepan or skillet and carefully pour some water into the pan around the bowls (about 2 1/2 inches deep). Be careful that the water does not get inside the bowls. Bring the water to boil, reduce the heat a bit, cover the saucepan, and allow the eggs to cook *au bain-marie* for about 7 to 8 minutes. When the eggs are ready, serve immediately.

This rather unpretentious dish could be served as a splendid introduction to a good dinner or simply, of itself, as a very nutritious lunch or light supper.

> *If Candlemas Day be fair and bright,*
> *Winter will have another flight;*
> *But if it be dark with clouds and rain,*
> *Winter is gone, and will not come again.*
> FOLK RHYME

ARTICHOKES GASCONNE STYLE
ARTICHAUTS A LA GASCONNE

4 servings

> **4 large artichokes, fresh**
> **juice of 1 lemon**
> **1 head leaf lettuce**
> **4 hard-boiled eggs**
> **1/2 cup herb vinaigrette (see page 215)**
> **green and black olives**
> **salt to taste**

1. Clean and trim the artichokes. Cook in lightly salted water mixed with the juice of the entire lemon for half an hour until the artichokes are soft and tender. Separate and discard the leaves, remove artichoke hearts, and chill for 1 hour.

2. Prepare the vinaigrette. Dip the artichoke hearts in the vinaigrette. Pour the remaining vinaigrette over the lettuce and toss.

3. Arrange the lettuce on four salad plates. Place each artichoke heart in the center of a bed of lettuce. Garnish by surrounding each artichoke heart with olives and slices of hard-boiled egg. Serve as an appetizer or in place of a salad.

 ou may use canned (drained) or frozen artichokes hearts in this recipe, in which case, chill the artichoke hearts and then proceed with step 2 of the recipe.

Good food should be grown on whole soil,
and be eaten whole, unprocessed, and garden fresh.

HELEN AND SCOTT NEARING
LIVING THE GOOD LIFE

LEEK TART
TARTE AUX POIREAUX

6 servings

Pastry shell *(la pâte brisée):*
  1 egg
  8 ozs flour (about 1 cup)
  1 stick sweet butter or margarine
  5 Tbsps ice water
  pinch of salt

Filling:
  2 lbs leeks
  3 eggs, lightly beaten
  1 cup white sauce (see page 207)
  8 ozs cream cheese
  salt and pepper to taste

1. Prepare white sauce.

2. Prepare the pastry shell by mixing the first five ingredients in a deep bowl. Use both a fork and your hands in mixing until the dough comes together. Do not overwork. Form a ball with the dough and sprinkle with flour. Let it rest in the refrigerator for 1 hour.

3. When the dough is ready to be worked, sprinkle sufficient flour over the table and gently roll the dough out, extending it in every direction. Using butter, thoroughly grease a tart pan or 8" or 9" pie dish and carefully place the rolled dough into it. The dough must be handled with the fingers at all times. Trim the edges in a decorative manner, cover the pastry shell with aluminum foil, and place in the oven at 250° F for about 12 minutes.

4. Wash and trim the leeks. Slice them two inches long and boil them for about 25 minutes. Drain them thoroughly.

5. Beat the eggs in a bowl, add the white sauce, cream cheese, leeks, and salt and pepper; blend everything together until it turns into a homogeneous mixture. Pour this mixture into the precooked tart or pie shell, smoothing it evenly with a fork. Bake at 350° F for about 30 minutes. Serve it hot or cold depending on the season. To serve cold, chill 1 hour or more.

Rice Bread
PAIN DE RIZ

6-8 servings

> 1 cup long-grain rice
> 2 cups water
> 3 to 4 Tbsps olive oil
> 4 tomatoes
> 1 onion
> 2/3 cup white sauce (see page 207)
> 3 eggs
> 1/3 cup grated Parmesan cheese
> mixed herbs (basil, thyme, rosemary)
> salt and pepper to taste

1. Cook the rice in boiling water. Add salt and lower the heat until the rice is cooked.

2. While the rice is cooking, wash and peel the tomatoes and onion. Pour a few tablespoons of olive oil into a skillet, and gently sauté the sliced tomatoes and onion. When the tomatoes begin to turn into a sauce, turn off the heat and cover the skillet until ready to use the sauce.

3. Prepare the white sauce.

4. Beat the eggs in a deep bowl. Add the white sauce, rice, tomato sauce, grated cheese, mixed herbs, salt, and pepper; mix completely.

5. Butter thoroughly a bread tin or a cake mold and pour the mixture into it. The mixture must cover about half of the bread tin. Place the tin in a roasting pan containing some water for baking the bread *au bain-marie*. Place the pan with the tin into the oven and bake at 350° F for about 35 to 40 minutes until the bread is firm. Take the bread out of the oven, allow it to cool for a few minutes, then unmold it onto a serving plate. This dish can be served hot during the cold-weather months, or refrigerate and serve cold during the summer.

Fennel With Lemon
Fenouil au Citron

4 servings

3 lbs fresh fennel
8 Tbsps olive oil
juice of 3 lemons
salt to taste
1/3 cup parsley, minced and chopped

1. Trim off and discard the stems of the fennel. Trim off and discard the outer skin. Cook the fennel in boiling, salty water for about 30 minutes. Drain and carefully cut them in halves.

2. Pour olive oil into a large skillet, add the fennel and the lemon juice. Cover the skillet and cook the fennel over low heat for about 10 minutes. Stir from time to time and see that there is ample oil to keep from burning. Taste before serving in case it needs more salt. Place the fennel in a serving dish and sprinkle the top with parsley as garnish.

Fennel, or finochio, as it is called by the Italians, is a rather popular vegetable in the southern countries of Europe. These days it is beginning to appear in American markets. This particular recipe goes well with a fish dish or any egg concoction.

O Thou, who kindly dost provide
For every creature's want!
We bless thee, God of Nature wide,
For all thy goodness lent;
And if it please thee, Heavenly Guide,
May never worse be sent;
But whether granted or denied,
Lord, bless us with content! Amen!

ROBERT BURNS "A GRACE BEFORE DINNER"

MUSHROOM SOUFFLÉ
SOUFFLÉ AUX CHAMPIGNONS DE PARIS

4-6 servings

1 cup white sauce
1 lb fresh mushrooms, sliced
1 onion, sliced
4 Tbsps butter
salt and pepper to taste
juice of 1 lemon
1 cup heavy cream
5 eggs, separated

1. Prepare white sauce following instructions on page 207.

2. Wash and thoroughly drain the mushrooms. Slice the mushrooms and the onion. Melt the butter in a frying pan and over medium-low heat, sauté the mushrooms and onion. Stir continuously. Remove the frying pan from the heat, add salt and pepper, lemon juice, and heavy cream; mix everything together very well. Place the frying pan back on the heat and continue to cook for about 3 minutes, stirring constantly. Take the pan off the heat and let it cool.

3. Separate the eggs. Put the whites aside. In a deep bowl, beat the egg yolks with a mixer. Add the white sauce and continue blending with the mixer. Add the mushroom sauce to the bowl, and blend all the ingredients thoroughly, using a fork.

4. With a mixer beat the egg whites in a separate bowl until stiff. Slowly fold the stiff egg whites into the mushroom mixture.

5. Preheat the oven to 350° F. Generously butter a soufflé dish and place the mushroom-egg mixture into the dish. Bake for about 20 to 25 minutes. When the soufflé is done, serve immediately.

LENTIL PÂTÉ
PÂTÉ DE LENTILLES

6 servings

> **2 cups brown or dark-green lentils**
> **2 large carrots, peeled and sliced**
> **1 onion, peeled and sliced**
> **water**
> **4 garlic cloves, minced**
> **1/2 cup heavy cream**
> **1/4 cup olive oil**
> **pinch of dried thyme**
> **salt and white pepper to taste**

1. In a good-sized saucepan, bring to boil the lentils, carrots, and onion in water to cover. Lower the flame to medium heat and cook for another 20 to 25 minutes until the vegetables are well done.

2. Drain the lentils and vegetables, saving the stock. Rinse the lentils and vegetables. Then pour them into a blender, add the garlic, heavy cream, olive oil, thyme, salt and pepper, and 1/2 cup of the stock (bouillon). Blend thoroughly, until mixture is smooth, and place in a buttered baking dish. Bake in oven at 350° F for about 30 minutes. It can be served hot or cold.

This delicious pâté can be served in many ways. It can be used as a spread, hot or cold, on top of crackers or thin slices of toasted French bread. It can also be served as an appetizer, again hot or cold. Or it can accompany the main dish as a side vegetable. In any case, it is something so tasty that most people rave about it.

> *Silence is the universal refuge, the sequel to all due discourses*
> *and all foolish acts, a balm to our every chagrin,*
> *as welcome after satiety as after disappointment.*
>
> HENRY DAVID THOREAU

Rice Casserole Italian Style
RISOTTO À L'ITALIENNE

4 servings

> **1 cup arborio rice**
> **3 cups water or vegetable broth**
> **1 lb frozen peas**
> **2 carrots, cut in julienne strips**
> **1 onion, well chopped**
> **1 cup dry white wine**
> **8 black olives, well chopped**
> **2 vegetable bouillon cubes**
> **4-oz jar of roasted peppers, chopped**
> **6 Tbsps olive oil**
> **1/2 tsp dried thyme**
> **1/4 tsp dried oregano**
> **salt and pepper to taste**
> **grated Parmesan cheese**

1. Combine all the ingredients except the cheese in a large saucepan and bring to a boil. Let it boil for about 5 minutes, then lower the heat, cover the saucepan, and let it simmer for about 20 minutes. Stir from time to time.

2. Butter sufficiently a large baking dish. Pour the contents of the saucepan into it, and add some more broth or water if it needs extra moisture. Bake in preheated oven at 300° F for about 30 minutes, stirring gently once or twice during the baking. The rice is ready when all the liquid has evaporated.

3. When the baking dish is out of the oven, sprinkle some grated cheese on top, and serve immediately while it is still hot.

It is a quick and simple way of preparing rice for a festive occasion, different from the monotonous everyday plain rice. This recipe contains all the magic, the aroma, and superb good taste expected in a dish that comes from the ancient Latin-Mediterranean part of the world.

POTATOES AU GRATIN
GRATIN DE POMMES DE TERRES

4-6 servings

1 large onion, chopped
6 cups boiled potatoes, diced
1/2 cup heavy cream
1 cup grated cheese of your choice
salt and pepper to taste
1 cup breadcrumbs
6 dots of butter

1. Place the onion and the potatoes in a large bowl. Mash and mix them well. Add the cream, the salt and pepper, 1/2 cup of grated cheese, and mix some more.

2. Place the mixture in a well-buttered baking dish and spread the remaining cheese on top. Cover the entire top with a thick layer of buttered breadcrumbs.

3. Bake in a preheated oven at 350° F for about 25 minutes. Serve immediately.

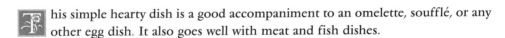 his simple hearty dish is a good accompaniment to an omelette, soufflé, or any other egg dish. It also goes well with meat and fish dishes.

OMELETTE WITH PEPPERS
OMELETTE AUX POIVRONS

4 servings

1 onion
1 sweet red pepper
1 sweet green pepper
2 Tbsps olive oil or butter
8 eggs
2 tsps cold water
salt and pepper to taste
6 Tbsps vegetable oil or butter

1. Peel and slice the onion thinly.

2. Wash and dry well the peppers, slicing them in round forms (rondelles).

3. Pour the 2 tablespoons of olive oil or butter into a frying pan, add the onion and peppers, and sauté slowly over a low heat for about 5 minutes. Cover and let simmer for a few minutes.

4. Break the eggs into a bowl, add the water, salt and pepper, and beat gently with a mixer.

5. Heat the 6 tablespoons of vegetable oil or butter in a large skillet. Let it get very hot; then pour the egg mixture into it and cook over medium-high heat. When the omelette is set on one side, turn it over quickly to the other side. Once that is accomplished, spread the onion and peppers over one-half of the omelette and fold it over with the other half. Serve the omelette in a hot dish.

PASTA WITH ZUCCHINI, LIMA BEANS, AND SUN-DRIED TOMATOES
PÂTES AUX LÉGUMES

4 servings

8 Tbsps olive oil
1 onion, coarsely chopped
1 medium-sized zucchini, quartered and sliced into small chunks
8 sun-dried tomato halves, cut into thin slices
2 garlic cloves, peeled and minced
3 Tbsps fresh basil leaves, chopped
salt and freshly ground pepper to taste
8 ozs pasta, penne or farfale
10-oz package lima beans
grated Parmesan cheese, as needed

1. Pour and heat the oil over medium flame in a good-sized skillet. Add the onion and sauté for about 3 minutes. Add the zucchini, tomatoes, garlic, basil, salt, and pepper; continue sautéing and stirring for about 8 minutes, until the vegetables become tender. Cover the skillet and keep the sauce hot.

2. Meanwhile, cook the pasta in boiling, salted water for about 3 minutes, add the frozen lima beans and continue cooking until the pasta is *al dente* and the beans are tender. Drain and place the pasta and beans in a large pasta bowl. Pour the sauce over it and toss well all ingredients. Serve hot, accompanied on the side by a small bowl of grated Parmesan cheese.

BRAISED BELGIAN ENDIVES
ENDIVES BRAISÉES

6 servings

12 heads of fresh Belgian endives
2 Tbsps lemon juice
4 Tbsps butter
1 cup water
2 Tbsps brown sugar (or white sugar)
salt to taste

1. Preheat the oven to 350° F. Wash the endives, removing any old leaves. Place them in a saucepan, add the water, lemon juice, sugar, and a pinch of salt. Cover the saucepan and bring the contents to a boil for about 5 minutes.

2. Butter a flat ovenproof dish, place the endives evenly in the dish, and pour the rest of the juice from the saucepan over them. Cover the dish with aluminum foil and bake the endives in the oven for about 45 minutes. Once or twice turn the endives around. They are ready when they have absorbed all their juice. Serve while they are hot.

Love is such a power that it makes all things to be shared.

THE CLOUD OF THE UNKNOWING

LEMON-SAFFRON FLAVORED RICE
RIZ AU SAFRAN

6-8 servings

1 onion, finely minced
1 red bell pepper, cut in small cubes
4 Tbsps olive oil
3 garlic cloves, well minced
2 cups long-grain rice
4 cups water
1 vegetable bouillon cube
1/8 tsp saffron
salt and pepper to taste
2 tsps grated lemon peel

1. Sauté the onion and the red pepper in the olive oil in a large skillet or frying pan for about 3 minutes. Add the rice and the garlic, mix will and continue to sauté over medium heat for about 1 minute. Stir continually.

2. Pour the water in a saucepan and bring to a boil. Add the rice and vegetable mixture, the bouillon, saffron, salt, and pepper. Mix the entire contents very well, stirring continually. Reduce heat and cook over medium heat for about 10 minutes. Cover the pan and let it simmer for about another 10 minutes over low heat until all the water is absorbed. Stir often.

3. When the rice is ready, add the grated lemon peel and mix well. Serve hot.

The saffron and the lemon peel give an exquisite aromatic flavor to this rice dish. This particular way of preparing the rice is rather traditional to northern Spain and southern France, where a flavorful rice is always a good accompaniment to seafood, eggs, or meat dishes.

To clasp the hands in prayer is the beginning of
an uprising against the disorder of the world.
KARL BARTH

SPINACH LASAGNA
LASAGNES MÉNAGÈRES AUX EPINARDS

4-6 servings

2 1/2 cups tomato sauce (see page 209)
1 lb lasagna noodles
1 Tbsp olive oil
1 large onion, chopped
1 lb mushrooms, washed and sliced
1 lb spinach, washed, chopped, and cooked
3 eggs, beaten
salt and pepper to taste
2 garlic cloves, minced
2 lbs ricotta cheese
1 lb grated mozzarella cheese
1/3 cup grated Romano cheese

1. Prepare the tomato sauce following the recipe on page 209 or use one of your preference. Be sure it contains 1 bay leaf and herbs.

2. Cook the lasagna noodles in a large saucepan, add olive oil and boil for 10 minutes. While the lasagna noodles are cooking, sauté in a good-sized skillet the onion and mushrooms for about 2 to 3 minutes. Add the spinach and the beaten eggs and continue to stir for another 2 to 3 minutes. Add salt and pepper according to taste.

3. Butter thoroughly a long flat baking dish (12" x 8") and spread the finely minced garlic on the bottom. Layer the tomato sauce, noodles, spinach mixture, and ricotta cheese. Repeat the layers a second time. Top with layer of noodles and tomato sauce and spread the mozzarella cheese evenly on the top. Bake at 350° F for 1 hour covered. Uncover the dish for the last 10 minutes. Take the lasagna out of the oven and let it cool for a few minutes. Sprinkle with some grated Romano cheese and serve while hot.

SHRIMP FRICASSEE
FRICASSÉE DE CREVETTES

4 servings

4 shallots, finely chopped
1/3 cup chives, finely chopped
1/3 cup parsley, finely chopped
1 1/2 lbs shrimp
5 Tbsps butter
salt and pepper to taste
pinch of cayenne pepper

1. Peel the shallots and chop finely. Chop also the chives and parsley.

2. Wash and clean the shrimp. Place the shrimp in a colander and drain thoroughly. Place them on a paper towel to dry.

3. Melt the butter in a frying pan. When the butter is hot, add the shrimp and fry for about 90 seconds. Add the shallots, chives, parsley, salt, pepper, and cayenne. Continue cooking for another 2 to 3 minutes. Stir continually until all blends well. Serve immediately, accompanied by slices of fresh French bread.

God, I have no idea where I am going. I do not see the road ahead of me. I cannot know for certain where it will end. Nor do I really know myself, and the fact that I think that I am following your will does not mean that I am actually doing so. But I believe that the desire to please You does in fact please you. And I hope I have the desire. And I know nothing about it. Therefore will I trust you always though I may seem to be lost and in the shadow of death, I will not fear, for you are ever with me, and you will never leave me to face my perils alone.

THOMAS MERTON

MASHED TURNIPS AND APPLES
PURÉE DE NAVETS ET POMMES

6 servings

4 large turnips
6 apples
2/3 cup dry white wine
butter
salt and pepper to taste

1. Peel the turnips and apples. Boil the turnips for 15 to 20 minutes alone in water in a good-sized pot. Then add the apples and boil both for another 10 minutes.

2. Once they are cooked, drain the turnips and apples and place them into a large bowl. Mash them thoroughly. Add the white wine, a chunk of butter, salt, and pepper. Mix well and pour into a buttered baking dish.

3. Bake in a preheated oven at 300° F for about 20 to 25 minutes. Serve hot.

POTATOES AU GRATIN FROM SAVOIE
LE GRATIN SAVOYARD

4 servings

1 1/2 cups milk
salt and white pepper to taste
3 Tbsps butter
2 lbs potatoes, peeled and thinly sliced
4 ozs grated Gruyère cheese

1. Mix the milk, salt, and pepper in a small saucepan and bring to a boil.

2. Butter an ovenproof deep casserole dish and pour in half the milk. Add the potato slices and arrange in a circle. Pour in the rest of the milk and cover the top entirely with the grated cheese.

3. Place the dish in the oven. Bake at 350° F until the potatoes are soft and the top looks golden brown. Serve immediately.

FAVA BEANS CASTILIAN STYLE

FÈVES À LA CASTILLANE

6-8 servings

12 ozs of fava beans (about 1 lb)
4 Tbsps butter
4 shallots, minced
2 garlic cloves, minced
1/4 cup fresh parsley, minced
2 vegetable bouillon cubes
1/2 cup olive oil
1 cup of Jerez wine or sherry
2 Tbsps dried or fresh tarragon
2 Tbsps dried or fresh savory
salt and pepper to taste

1. Wash and rinse the beans. Place them in a large saucepan filled with water. Cover the pan and cook the beans over medium heat for 25 to 30 minutes. Do not allow the beans to overcook. They must be tender yet remain firm. Drain them.

2. Heat the butter in a saucepan over moderate heat. Add the shallots, garlic, and fresh parsley. Sauté for one minute. Add the fava beans, bouillon cubes, oil, Jerez wine, tarragon, savory, salt, and pepper. Cook over low heat, stirring often, for about 5 minutes.

3. Grease an earthenware tureen and pour the contents of the saucepan into it. Cover and place the tureen in a preheated oven and bake at 350° F for 20 minutes. Serve hot.

Joy is the most infallible sign of the presence of God.
TEILHARD DE CHARDIN

Split Peas Saint Honoré Country Style

PETITS POIS PAYSANNE SAINT-HONORÉ

4-6 servings

4 cups water
1 lb dried split peas (or dried whole peas)
1 cup small onions, peeled
1 small head of lettuce, finely chopped
4 Tbsps butter
salt and pepper to taste
2 Tbsps brown sugar
3 Tbsps flour

1. Pour the water into a large pan, add the peas, onions, lettuce, butter, and some salt. Bring the water to a boil. Reduce heat to a medium-low flame and cook for about 30 minutes. Stir occasionally.

2. When the peas are done, add the flour and sugar to the casserole dish to make a sauce with the juice that is left over from the cooking. The liquid remaining should be just enough to make the sauce. Turn off the heat, cover the casserole, and allow to sit for 10 minutes before serving. Serve hot.

This dish is a complete meal in itself. In our monastery we frequently serve it with a side portion of rice or some cooked vegetable. In France, they sometimes add (at the very end of cooking) a few tablespoons of heavy cream. The combination of the lettuce and the sugar, sweet-sour, give the peas a distinct taste of their own.

Six years you shall sow your field, and six years you shall prune your vineyard, and gather in its fruits; but in the seventh year there shall be a sabbath of solemn rest for the land, a sabbath to the Lord; you shall not sow your field or prune your vineyard. What grows itself in your harvest you shall not reap, and the grapes of your undressed vine you shall not gather; it shall be a year of solemn rest for the land.

LEVITICUS 25:3–5 (RSV)

SALADS

BEAN SPROUT SALAD
SALADE DE GERMES DE SOJA

4 servings

For the salad:
- 1 lb soybean sprouts
- 2 sweet red peppers, diced
- 1 cucumber, diced
- 8 chives, finely cut and minced

For the dressing:
- 4 Tbsps olive oil
- 1 Tbsp vinegar
- 2 tsps soy sauce
- 1 tsp mustard
- pinch of sugar
- pinch of salt

1. Wash and rinse the bean sprouts. Place them in a deep bowl and add the diced peppers, cucumber, and chives.

2. Mix together the oil, vinegar, soy sauce, mustard, sugar, and salt. Pour over the salad and mix thoroughly. Serve immediately.

WHITE SALAD
SALADE BLANCHE

6 servings

- 2 medium-large size heads of cauliflower, cut into flowerets
- 3 medium-sized cucumbers, peeled and sliced
- 4 shallots, thinly chopped
- 3 Tbsps fresh parsley, chopped
- vinaigrette (see page 214)

1. Place the cauliflower flowerets in a large pan with salted water. Let them boil for about 4 to 6 minutes. Don't overcook them for they must remain firm. Drain and rinse under cold water; drain again thoroughly.

2. Place the cauliflower flowerets in a deep bowl, add the cucumbers, which have been cut in four lengthwise and then sliced, and the finely chopped shallots. Refrigerate for at least 2 hours.

3. Just before serving, prepare and add the vinaigrette, sprinkle with the freshly chopped parsley, mix well, and serve cold.

SALAD OF JERUSALEM ARTICHOKES
SALADE DE TOPINAMBOURS

4-6 servings

1 lb Jerusalem artichokes
1 large fresh carrot
3 shallots
2 medium-sized fresh turnips
1/3 cup parsley, chopped and minced
6 Tbsps olive oil
2 tsps lemon juice
1 tsp dry white wine
salt and pepper to taste
pinch of dry mustard (optional)

1. Wash and peel the vegetables. Pass them through a shredder. Place them in a salad bowl and refrigerate for at least 1 hour.

2. Before serving, add the chopped parsley, oil, lemon juice, wine, salt, and pepper. Mix thoroughly and serve cold.

Regard all utensils of the monastery
as if they were the sacred vessels of the altar.
RULE OF SAINT BENEDICT

Mixed Salad
SALADE MÉLANGÉE

6-8 servings

1 head Boston lettuce
1 head bibb or leaf lettuce
1 medium-sized head of radicchio
4 medium-sized Belgian endives
1 bunch arugula
1 bunch watercress
vinaigrette (see page 214)
salt and pepper to taste
chopped chives and chervil (optional)

1. Wash the greens thoroughly and separate the individual leaves. Do not cut or split the leaves, only the stems. Drain the leaves completely, roll them with paper towels and refrigerate until ready to serve. This will allow them to remain fresh and crisp.

2. Just before serving the salad, arrange the greens in a salad bowl and mix them. Prepare a simple vinaigrette, pour this over the greens, and toss lightly. Sprinkle with some finely chopped chives and/or chervil, if you wish.

Salads like this one are part of the daily fare of ordinary French homes. They may not always contain such a variety of greens, but whatever they are made of, they never cease to appeal to the French palate, especially after a good main course. And, of course, a green salad is de rigueur to wash out the palate before the dessert!

CARROT SALAD BONAPARTE
SALADE DE CAROTTES BONAPARTE

4 servings

1 lb carrots, grated
2 bell peppers, one red and one green, sliced julienne style
4 scallions, thinly sliced
1 small box of sweet light raisins (optional)
4 Tbsps walnut oil
2 Tbsps cider vinegar or sherry vinegar
salt to taste
finely chopped parsley as garnish

1. Wash, dry, and peel the vegetables. Grate or slice them as indicated above.

2. In a salad bowl, mix the oil, vinegar, and salt. Add carrots, peppers, scallions, and raisins. Mix and toss the salad. Sprinkle some finely chopped parsley on the top and serve.

SALAD SAINT MARY MAGDALENE
SALADE SAINTE MARIE-MADELEINE

4 servings

1 bunch fresh arugula leaves
1 bunch fresh mâche leaves
1 medium-sized red onion, thinly sliced
4 Tbsps virgin olive oil
1 Tbsp balsamic vinegar
1 small goat cheese (about 4 ozs)
salt and pepper to taste
vinaigrette (see page 214)

1. Wash and drain the arugula and mâche leaves. Discard the tough stems and place the leaves in a salad bowl. Add the sliced onion.

2. Warm the goat cheese in the oven at 300° F for about 5 to 6 minutes. Meanwhile, prepare the vinaigrette, mixing the ingredients well. Pour the vinaigrette over the salad. Toss and blend well. Serve the salad on individual salad plates. Crumble the warm cheese on top of each serving. Serve immediately.

Mushroom Salad With Lemon
Salade de Champignons au Citron

4-6 servings

For the salad:
    1 1/2 lbs fresh mushrooms
    1 head bibb or Boston lettuce
    1 onion
    1/2 cup fresh parsley, minced
    fresh radishes, thinly sliced (optional)

For the vinaigrette:
    6 Tbsps olive oil (add more if needed)
    3 Tbsps lemon juice (add more if needed)
    salt and pepper to taste

1. Wash and drain the mushrooms thoroughly. Cut them in thin slices and place them in a salad bowl. Refrigerate for at least one hour until ready to serve.

2. Separate the lettuce leaves. Wash and drain them thoroughly. Refrigerate until ready to be served. Cut the onion in very thin slices and place them in a container with hot water for about 3 minutes to take the sting away. Rinse and drain them completely.

3. Prepare vinaigrette by mixing together the olive oil, lemon juice, salt, and pepper.

4. Just before serving, take the mushrooms out of the refrigerator, add the onion, parsley, radishes, and the vinaigrette; mix the salad well. Prepare a bed of lettuce on each plate to be served; spread the mushroom mixture evenly on top in a decorative fashion. Serve cold.

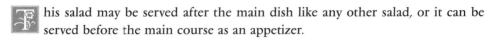 his salad may be served after the main dish like any other salad, or it can be served before the main course as an appetizer.

To be a witness does not consist in engaging in propaganda nor even in stirring people up, but in being a living mystery. It means to live in such a way that one's life would not make sense if God did not exist.

Cardinal Suhard

DESSERTS

ENGLISH CREAM
CRÈME ANGLAISE

4-6 servings

1 qt whole milk
1 tsp vanilla extract
pinch of salt
6 egg yolks, well beaten
1/2 cup granulated sugar

1. Combine the milk with the vanilla extract in a good-sized saucepan and bring it to a boil.

2. Combine the egg yolks with the sugar and salt in a mixing bowl and beat thoroughly with a mixer. Little by little and rather slowly, pour the warm milk into the egg mixture while continuing to stir with the mixer. It must blend thoroughly.

3. Place the entire mixture into the saucepan and begin to cook over medium-low heat. Continue to stir until the cream begins to thicken. Do not let it boil. Pour the cream into a chilled bowl, stir once or twice, cover and refrigerate until it is time to serve.

This is a useful recipe for almost any basic dessert. It can be chilled and served alone or combined with fruits or other desserts, such as Oeufs à la neige (Snowy Eggs, see recipe on page 92). Lemon or orange rind, instant coffee, ground cinnamon, or melted chocolate can be infused in the milk to change the flavoring of the custard cream.

"Help us to find God," the disciples asked the elder.
"No one can help you do that," the elder said.
"Why not?" the disciples asked amazed.
"For the same reason that no one can help fish to find the ocean."

UNKNOWN

FLOATING ISLAND
ÎLE FLOTTANTE
6 servings

For the meringue:
   6 egg whites
   2 ozs sugar
   1/3 cup roasted almonds, chopped finely
   pinch of salt
   Crème Anglaise (see page 42)

For the caramel:
   6 Tbsps sugar
   3 Tbsps water
   1 drop cider vinegar

1. In a deep bowl, beat the egg whites stiff, adding little by little the salt, sugar, and finely chopped almonds. Butter thoroughly a one-quart mold and pour the meringue into it, filling about three-fourths of the mold. Place the mold in a large baking dish with water to cook it *au bain-marie*. Make sure not a drop of water gets into the meringue. Place the baking dish with the mold into the oven. Cook slowly at 300° F for about 25 minutes.

2. While the meringue is in the oven, prepare Crème Anglaise.

3. When it is time to serve, unmold the meringue upside down with great care onto a serving plate. Pour the Crème Anglaise all around it. Combine sugar, vinegar, and a bit of water into a saucepan, stirring over low-medium heat until the mixture turns brown to make a quick caramel, and pour immediately over the dessert. This dessert is usually served cold, which means the Crème Anglaise is prepared earlier and refrigerated before serving.

FLAN WITH PEARS
FLAN AUX POIRES

6 servings

> **1/2 cup flour**
> **3/4 cup sugar**
> **1 small (1/4 oz) package dry yeast**
> **2 eggs, separated**
> **2 cups milk**
> **4 Tbsps butter**
> **1 lb pears, peeled and sliced (about 6)**
> **1 vanilla bean**

1. In a deep bowl, mix the flour, sugar, and yeast. Add the egg yolks and the milk. Melt the butter in a small casserole and add to the mixture. Stir continually by hand or with the help of a mixer.

2. In a separate bowl, beat the egg whites stiff and gradually add them to the flour mixture.

3. Butter thoroughly a long (8" x 12" x 2") baking dish and pour the mixture into it. Cover the entire top of the dish with the sliced pears. Place the dish in the oven at 350° F for 45 minutes. Sprinkle some confectioners' sugar on the flan before serving.

Blessed is he that had preserved this good seed when it fell in his soul, and has made it to increase without destroying it by idle things and by the distractions of that which is transitory.

ISAAC OF NINEVEH

Soufflé of the Dawn
Soufflé l'Aurore

4 servings

6 Tbsps diced fresh fruit (strawberries, raspberries, blackberries)
1/4 cup Grand-Marnier
4 Tbsps butter, melted
1/4 cup flour
1/2 qt whole milk
2 tsps vanilla extract
1/2 cup sugar, plus extra for coating soufflé dish
5 egg yolks
4 egg whites

1. Dice the fruit very small. Place it in a small deep bowl and pour the Grand-Marnier over it. Mix well.

2. Melt half the butter in a good-sized saucepan, add the flour and stir continuously. In a separate pan, bring the milk to a boil, then add to the flour mixture. Add the vanilla and the sugar and continue to stir until this mixture comes to a boil. Remove the saucepan from the heat.

3. Beat the egg yolks and the egg whites separately. Gradually add the egg yolks to the milk and flour mixture, beating with a mixer continuously at a low speed. Melt the rest of the butter. Then add the butter, fruit, and egg whites, beating (at low speed) continuously.

4. Butter a deep soufflé dish and then sprinkle with sugar to coat the entire dish. Pour the soufflé mixture into the dish, filling about 3 quarts of it, and leave the remaining space for the soufflé to rise. Place the dish in the oven at 350° F for about 25 to 30 minutes. Serve immediately as it comes out of the oven.

> *Let us not despair. Let us not lose faith in people and certainly not in God. We must believe that a prejudiced mind can be changed, and that people, by the grace of God, can be lifted from the valley of hate to the high mountain of love.*
>
> Martin Luther King

BASQUE CAKE WITH PEARS
GÂTEAU BASQUE AUX POIRES

8 servings

For the cake:
 2 cups flour
 1 1/2 tsps baking powder
 4 Tbsps sugar (or molasses)
 1 cup milk
 2 Tbsps pear liqueur (or another liqueur of your preference)
 2 eggs
 6 pears, peeled, cored, and thinly sliced

For the topping:
 1/2 cup butter (or margarine)
 1 cup confectioners' sugar
 1 Tbsp pear liqueur (or pure vanilla extract)

1. Combine the flour, baking powder, and sugar in a deep bowl and mix well. In another bowl, beat the milk, pear liqueur, and eggs thoroughly with a mixer.

2. Combine the flour mixture and egg mixture. Stir by hand until all is equally moist. Spoon the batter into a well-buttered and floured long baking dish that is 2" deep; cover the top with the sliced pears. Bake in a preheated oven at 350° F for about 45 minutes.

3. Prepare the topping by mixing the butter, confectioners' sugar, and pear liqueur; beat until it becomes thoroughly creamed. When the cake is done, remove from the oven and while it is still hot, spread the topping over the entire surface. Allow it to cool and then serve.

The future enters into us, in order to transform
itself in us, long before it happens.
RAINER MARIA RILKE

Apple Flan Alsatian Style

FLAN AUX POMMES ALSACIEN

6 servings

2 lbs apples (about 8)
5 eggs
3 ozs sugar
2 cups milk
4 Tbsps butter, melted
2 ozs raisins

1. Peel and slice the apples. Spread them evenly across the bottom of a well-buttered baking dish.

2. Break the eggs into a deep bowl and add the sugar. Beat with a mixer or by hand. While mixing, add the milk, little by little. Then add the melted butter and raisins.

3. Pour the mixture evenly over the apples and bake at 350° F for about 45 minutes. Serve lukewarm.

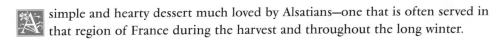 simple and hearty dessert much loved by Alsatians—one that is often served in that region of France during the harvest and throughout the long winter.

He sendeth sun, he sendeth shower.
Alike they're needful to the flower;
And joys and tears alike are sent
To give the soul fit nourishment.
As comes to me or cloud or sun.
Father! thy will, not mine, be done.

SARAH FLOWER ADAMS

BURNT CREAM
CRÉME BRULÉE

4 servings

> 1/3 cup sugar
> 1/4 cup boiling water
> 1 Tbsp cornstarch
> 2 cups milk
> 4 egg yolks
> 1 tsp vanilla extract
> 1 Tbsp cognac
> 1 small piece of lemon rind

1. Heat the sugar in a good-sized frying pan until it begins to caramelize. Add the water immediately and stir continually until it becomes a syrup.

2. Mix thoroughly in a cup the cornstarch and 4 tablespoons of milk. Scald the rest of the milk.

3. Beat the egg yolks and place them in a double boiler with the water already boiling. Immediately add the cornstarch mixture; then add the scalded milk gradually while stirring continually. Add the caramel syrup very slowly, then the lemon rind, vanilla, and cognac; continue cooking the cream over the boiling water. Stir continually until it thickens. Remove from the heat, place it in a serving dish or in individual dessert glasses, and chill in the refrigerator for a few hours before serving. Serve very cold.

According to a Spanish proverb, four persons are wanted to make a good salad: a spendthrift for oil, a miser for vinegar, a counselor for salt, and a madman to stir it all up.

ABRAHAM HAYWARD, *THE ART OF DINING*

Galette From Nantes With Almonds

Galette Nantaise aux Amandes

4 to 6 servings

1 oz (4 envelopes) active dry yeast
6 Tbsps water, lukewarm
8 Tbsps butter, preferably sweet, melted
2 eggs, lightly beaten
1/3 cup almonds, crushed and pulverized
1 lemon rind, finely grated
1 Tbsp rum
1/2 cup sugar
pinch of salt
2 cups flour
confectioner's sugar
butter

1. Dissolve the yeast in the lukewarm water and pour into a large mixing bowl. Add the melted butter, eggs, almonds, lemon rind, rum, sugar, and salt. Mix well.

2. Gently add the flour, little by little, and beat with the electric mixer. Roll the dough on a floured table or board, and knead until it becomes smooth. Roll back the mixture and form into a ball.

3. Place the ball in a mixing bowl and sprinkle with flour. Cover the bowl with a kitchen towel and leave in a warm place for 1 1/2 to 2 hours.

4. Roll out the dough on a floured table and form a circle. Place the circle carefully in a well-buttered baking sheet. Form a rim around the edge, sprinkle confectioner's sugar over the top and dot with butter. Heat the oven to 450° F and bake the galette for no more than 7 minutes. Serve warm. (One may also serve with sweet yogurt, crème chantilly, or fresh cream if preferred.)

LIGHT WAFFLES

GAUFRES MOLLES

8-10 waffles

> 1 3/4 cups flour
> 3 Tbsps sugar
> 1 Tbsp vanilla
> 1 small (1/4 oz) package yeast powder
> 4 eggs, separated
> pinch of salt
> 7 Tbsps butter, melted
> 2/3 cup milk
> 1 cup heavy cream

1. Place the flour in a deep bowl, add the sugar, vanilla, yeast, egg yolks, salt, and melted butter. Add the milk and then mix vigorously with a wooden spatula or with the help of an electric mixer. Allow the mixture to rest in a warm place for at least 1 hour.

2. Beat the egg whites and whip the heavy cream separately. Fold the beaten eggs and the whipped cream carefully into the flour mixture. Cook the waffles in a waffle iron for about 50 to 60 seconds each. Serve the waffles with fruit jam or syrup.

SPRING

Come then, my love,
My lovely one, Winter is past,
The rains are over and gone,
The flowers appear on the earth,
The season of glad songs has come.

SONG OF SONGS 2:10

ere in the northeastern United States, the long night of winter usually begins to withdraw sometime during the month of March. Winter does not yield its territory easily, however; snowstorms can appear in late April and on high, remote ground there can be freezing temperatures well into May. In spite of all the weather games encountered during the uncertain transition of seasons at this time of year, deep inside we come to know that at least the worst of winter is gone for another year and spring is finally here to stay.

Spring is a time of growth, a season full of promises. The magic of the early spring rains and the warm rays of the sun marvelously renew the earth's plants and all living creatures. There is nothing so glorious to contemplate at this time as the gradual greening of the pasture fields. Under the nurture of the rains and the warming of the sun, the fresh new tender green appears slowly in the meadows—what a sight that is on a clear day with the sun high above! We know for sure that spring is here when, taking a long walk in the woodlands, we see the trees turning green as well.

In the variable weather of the early springtime, snow may appear briefly on the ground and then disappear the next day in warm sunshine. There are days of heavy rain and days when the wind blows gusty and strong across the ground. Early spring, unlike any other transition period between seasons, is a strange, seductive time. It evokes in us all sorts of feelings and emotions....

As we approach more deeply the heart of the spring season, the clear azure skies will be filled with flocks of birds returning from the south, finches, wrens, bluebirds, orioles, and the like. At dawn and sunset we can hear the Canada geese honking their way back north from the southern regions where they have wintered. From the wetlands and marshes emerge frogs, toads, and spring peepers, all of them joyous in release from winter hibernation. The early spring flowers appear in the gardens and the fields. Here at our monastery in upstate New York, the daffodils have been naturalized over the years throughout the property, and it is an uplifting sight to see them blossom in profusion for several weeks. The other early spring flowers—crocuses, small anemones, windflowers, Japanese irises, tulips—are also a sight to behold. They cheer the heart of every gardener and all others who come to envy them.

To me, nothing expresses so vividly the reality of spring as the tiny seed that lies buried through the long bleak night of winter, waiting to be awakened from its long sleep. With the arrival of spring, its first tiny leaf suddenly emerges above ground, radiant with new life. The metamorphosis taking place in the small seed parallels the daily transformation in our own lives. At one time or another, we all pass through the night of winter. We experience the slow decline followed by the rising, with the arrival of spring and its burst of new life within us.

For myself, springtime is preeminently a time for planting, as it is for all those who are dedicated to the cultivation of the land. (Monks traditionally throughout the centuries have been watchful stewards of their land and avid cultivators of gardens.) It is always advantageous to start early in the garden, as soon as the soil is workable and warm enough to expedite germination. But before planting, of course, there is the annual cleanup and the raking off of winter's debris to be done. The compost pile must also be transported to the future vegetable garden and mixed with the soil. Once this chore is accomplished, I start planting the early spring vegetables. The sooner plants begin to grow, the quicker they develop a strong root system which collects the soil moisture and soil nutrients necessary to help develop healthy plants and excellent yields. However, as careful gardeners, we must be extremely vigilant during this time to see that the early vegetable and flower seedlings are not hurt by a late frost. Here in the northeast, most gardeners and farmers agree that the danger of frost remains until the middle of May, and in some areas further north, even up to the end of May. For that reason many gardeners will not set their tomatoes, peppers, corn, eggplants, or cucumbers in the ground outside until the traditional Memorial Day weekend.

Gardening is both a task and an art that we learn to fathom through the experience of the years. It is important that at first we start slowly and follow through gradually. Mother Nature herself should be our guide. Her signals indicate the propitious time for many of the early spring chores to be done:

- When the crocus is in bloom, start the cleanup of winter's debris.
- When the forsythia blooms, prune the roses, the evergreens, and other plants that may have been damaged by the weather.

- When the soil warms up, sow lettuce, radishes, spinach, arugula, leeks, chard, and sweetpeas. (In many monasteries the first sweetpeas are planted on March 25, the feast of the Annunciation.) Begin to divide and transplant the perennials.

- Towards the middle of May (in the northeast), sow corn, beans, cucumbers, and squash.

- On Memorial Day weekend, transplant into the garden the seedlings of tomatoes, basil, peppers, and eggplant. Plant the annuals in the flower garden.

Spring coincides with the yearly celebration of Lent, Holy Week, and Easter. Lent allows us to face all the grim aspects of our lives and points us toward the joyful hope of new Easter life. In monasteries, where Lenten fasting and penance tends to be rather sober in nature, the joy of Resurrection knows no bounds. It is the most thrilling and uplifting experience of the liturgical year. The bells ring with alleluias, the chapel is clothed with flowers and bright lights, the chant echoes the joy of Christ's Resurrection, as both monks and nuns greet one another with the traditional "Christ is risen" and its reply, "Indeed, He is risen."

Since the feast of the Resurrection is one feast found in most religious traditions, we should really let ourselves dance in this planetary festival of rejoicing. The new life of spring, the springing up of flowers in our gardens, is realized most fully in the springing up of the divine life in the inner depths of our hearts. In this country, the Easter Lily (Madonna Lily) has become the symbol of resurrection, the promise of new life. The lily is often used in the Old and New Testaments to portray beauty, perfection, goodness, and godliness—ideals that we all could strive to incorporate in our daily lives. Thus, spring, and the mysteries celebrated during the season, brings us from sorrow and death to the affirmation of hope and the experience of the renewal of life in our daily existence.

> *If we had no winter, the spring would not be so pleasant; if we did not sometimes taste of adversity, prosperity would not be so welcome.*
>
> ANNE BRADSTREET

Soups and Appetizers

SPRING SOUP
POTAGE PRINTANIER

6 servings

3 Tbsps butter or margarine
2 cups cauliflower, chopped
2 carrots, sliced
1 cup fresh peas
2 leeks, chopped
1 cup spinach, chopped
1 celeriac root, peeled and chopped
2 qts water
1 cup sherry wine
3 vegetable bouillon cubes
2 tomatoes, peeled and diced
pinch of mixed herbs (parsley, chervil, thyme are suggested)
salt and pepper to taste

1. Melt the butter in a soup pot and sauté all the vegetables, except the tomatoes, for one minute or two.

2. Add the water, sherry, bouillon cubes, tomatoes, mixed herbs, salt, and pepper. Cook the soup slowly over medium-low heat for about 1 hour. Stir from time to time and add some water if need be. Simmer for 10 minutes.

3. When the soup is done, sprinkle with some more fresh, finely chopped herbs and serve immediately.

Over the land freckled with snow half thawed
The speculating rooks at their nest cawed,
And saw from elm-tops, delicate as flower of grass,
What we below could not see.
Winter pass.

EDWARD THOMAS

RICE SOUP
POTAGE AU RIZ

4 servings

4 Tbsps butter (or oil)
1 cup long-grain rice
7 cups boiling water
1 large carrot, thinly grated
1 small onion, diced
1 green pepper, diced
5 Tbsps chopped, fresh parsley
salt and pepper to taste
pinch of saffron

1. Melt the butter or oil in a good-sized soup pot and add to it the rice, stirring it continually for a minute or two in the melted butter.

2. Add immediately 7 cups of boiling water, the carrot, onion, green pepper, and parsley.

3. Cook the soup over a low flame for about 30 to 40 minutes, until the rice is tender. Add salt and pepper, and a sprinkle of saffron for a bit of extra aroma and taste. Simmer for 10 minutes and serve it hot.

A very simple and light soup, easy to make and most appetizing on a cool day. Serve it with French bread.

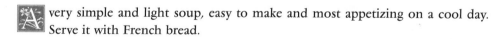

Lift up your heart to Him, sometimes even at your meals, and when you are in company; the least little remembrance will always be acceptable to Him. You need not cry very hard; he is nearer than we are aware of.

BROTHER LAWRENCE

FARMER'S SOUP
SOUPE DE LA FERME

6 servings

- 4 large carrots
- 3 potatoes
- 2 parsnips
- 3 large onions
- 4 ozs butter or margarine
- 4 Tbsps flour
- 3 qts water (add additional water if need be)
- 1 qt dry white wine
- 2 vegetable bouillon cubes
- salt and pepper to taste
- 3 Tbsps minced fresh parsley

1. Peel and slice the vegetables. Mince the carrots, celery, and onion. In a large soup kettle, brown the vegetables in the butter for a few minutes. Sprinkle the flour over the vegetables and mix thoroughly.

2. Immediately after mixing the flour and vegetables, pour in the water and wine. Add the bouillon cubes, salt and pepper, and cook the soup slowly over medium heat for about 90 minutes. Add more water if necessary. The kettle should be covered during the cooking time. At the end, add the thinly cut and minced parsley, let it simmer for about 10 minutes, and then serve while the soup is hot.

This recipe originally came from Burgundy, where the farmers are used to plenty of meat and wine in their regional cooking. While nonvegetarians may wish to put some meat into the soup both for taste and flavor, the vegetarians can easily substitute tofu or something similar. In our small monastery we prepare the soup as presented here, without meat in it.

TOMATO LENTIL SOUP
SOUPE DE LENTILLES

6-8 servings

1 cup brown or green lentils
3 qts water (add more if desired)
1 large onion, sliced
2 large carrots, cut very fine
2 celery stalks, cut fine
2 large potatoes, peeled and diced
1 turnip, diced
4 garlic cloves, minced
1 bunch of spinach leaves or sorrel
6 Tbsps olive oil
1 cup tomato sauce (8 ozs)
1 bay leaf
salt and pepper to taste
1/2 cup long-grain rice
pinch of powdered cumin (optional)

1. Wash and rinse the lentils and place them in a large soup pot. Add the water, the sliced vegetables, and the rest of the ingredients except the salt and pepper. Bring the mixture to a boil. Then lower the flame to medium heat and cook slowly for 1 hour.

2. When the soup is done, add the salt and pepper, let the soup simmer over low heat for a short while and serve while hot. Remove bay leaf before serving.

This is a nutritious soup for all-year-round serving, especially in early spring when one may gather fresh sorrel from one's garden or from the local market as they do in France. While the sorrel will give a tart, bitter taste to the soup, the carrot's sweetness will compensate, creating a marvelous, unique blended flavor.

It is always Spring in the Soul united to God.
SAINT JEAN MARIE VIANNEY

CREAM OF SORREL SOUP
POTAGE À L'OSEILLES

4-6 servings

6 Tbsps olive oil or butter
2 leeks, well chopped (only the white part of the leek)
1 large onion, well chopped
8 ozs coarsely chopped sorrel (about 5 cups)
1/2 lb potatoes, peeled and cubed
6 cups water (add a bit more if needed)
3 vegetable bouillon cubes
1 bunch of parsley, well chopped and minced
salt and pepper to taste
6 Tbsps heavy cream

1. In a large stainless steel saucepan, sauté in olive oil the leek and onion lightly. Add the sorrel and potatoes and stir for a few minutes until the vegetables are well blended.

2. Add the water, bouillon cubes, parsley, salt, and pepper; boil for about 15 minutes. Turn down the heat and simmer in the covered saucepan for about 20 to 25 minutes more.

3. Pass the soup through the blender at a high speed until thoroughly blended and then pour it back into the pan. Add the heavy cream and stir the soup. Reheat the soup and serve hot.

orrel soup is a treat any time of the year and very popular in France during the spring, when this vegetable is in season. If sorrel is not available, substitute Swiss chard or spinach, though none of them have the light sour taste sorrel has that makes it so appealing to the taste. Sorrel grows easily in our monastery herb garden and, being a perennial, it returns invariably each year.

To be without a sense of taste is to be deficient in an exquisite faculty, that of appreciating the qualities of food, just as a person may lack the faculty of appreciating the quality of a book or a work of art. It is to want a vital sense, one of the elements of human superiority.

GUY DE MAUPASSANT

ENDIVE SOUP FROM THE ARDENNES
SOUPE ARDENNAISE À L'ENDIVE

4 servings

> **4 medium potatoes**
> **2 leeks, white parts only**
> **2 shallots**
> **2 Belgian endives**
> **4 Tbsps butter**
> **5 cups whole or low-fat milk (more if needed)**
> **salt and white pepper to taste**
>   **(cayenne pepper may be substituted for white pepper)**
> **freshly ground nutmeg to taste**
> **a few croutons for each soup dish**

1. Wash and peel the potatoes. Cut them in thin slices. Slice the leeks, shallots, and endives finely.

2. Melt the butter in a saucepan. Add the leeks, shallots, and endives and sauté them for a few minutes. Add the milk and bring to a light boil. Add the potatoes, salt, pepper, and nutmeg. Lower the heat to medium-low and cook the soup for about 12 minutes, stirring from time to time.

3. After 12 minutes, turn off the heat, cover the saucepan with a lid, and allow the soup to sit for 20 minutes.

4. Grill a few pieces of bread cubes to use as croutons. Place a few in each plate and pour the soup on top. Serve hot.

This is a fine soup from the northern region of France—endive country. The endive gives a particularly light taste to the soup. Those who may wish to accentuate the taste a bit further may sprinkle some grated cheese or crème fraîche on top of the soup.

Split-Pea Soup Saint Germain
Potage Saint-Germain

6-8 servings

1 lb dried yellow split peas (green may be substituted)
2 medium-sized carrots, peeled and diced
2 potatoes, peeled and diced
1 celery stalk, diced
1 medium-sized turnip, diced
2 medium onions, sliced in small pieces
bay leaf
3 vegetable bouillon cubes
6 Tbsps olive oil or butter
salt and pepper to taste
croutons
cayenne pepper (optional)

1. Soak the peas for 3 to 4 hours and drain them. Fill a large soup kettle with water and bring to a boil. Add the peas, vegetables, bay leaf, and bouillon cubes. Cook over medium heat for about 1 hour. Stir from time to time. Let it cool.

2. Remove the bay leaf from the soup. Put the soup in a blender and blend until it turns into a smooth cream. Pour soup back into the kettle and add the oil or butter, salt and pepper to taste, cayenne pepper if desired, and extra water or milk according to preference. Bring it back to a boil, stirring continually. Let it simmer for 10 minutes. Place the croutons in the individual soup plates and pour the soup on top of them. Serve hot.

his recipe is one of the many monastic variations on this very traditional and classical French soup. On festive occasions, one can add a large tablespoon of dry sherry to each plate for a bit of extra taste. It is delicious. If you add the sherry, omit the cayenne pepper.

Russian Beet Soup

BORTSCH

6 servings

2 red beets
2 carrots
2 potatoes
2 leeks
1/2 head red cabbage
8 mushrooms
1 onion
4 tomatoes, peeled
3 1/2 qts water
4 Tbsps vegetable oil
salt and pepper
heavy cream or crème fraîche (see page 213)
parsley or fennel leaves, finely minced

1. Wash and peel the beets, carrots, and potatoes. Dice them in small cubes. Slice the leeks, cabbage, mushrooms, onion, and tomatoes in small pieces.

2. In a large soup pot bring the water to boil, then add the oil and all the vegetables. Cover and cook the soup over medium heat for about 30 minutes. Add salt and pepper to the soup, stir it, and let it simmer for 15 minutes over low heat.

3. Serve the soup hot, adding 1 tablespoon heavy cream or crème fraîche, and some minced parsley or fennel leaves to the center of each dish of soup.

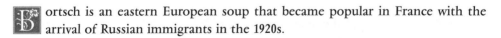

ortsch is an eastern European soup that became popular in France with the arrival of Russian immigrants in the 1920s.

SAINT ODO'S SOUP
SOUPE SAINT-ODO

4-6 servings

4 Tbsps olive oil
2 medium-sized onions, finely chopped
3 tomatoes, peeled and coarsely chopped
2 medium-sized zucchini, quartered lengthwise,
    and then slice in small chunks
1 cup peas, fresh or frozen
1 celery branch, thinly sliced
7 cups water or broth (of your preference)
1 tsp thyme (fresh or dried)
2 Tbsps parsley (fresh)
2 Tbsps fresh basil, chopped
6 Tbsps barley
salt and freshly ground pepper to taste

1. Pour the oil into a soup kettle. Add the onion and tomatoes; cook over low heat until the vegetables wilt and turn into a sauce. Stir from time to time.

2. Stir in the zucchini, peas, celery, water, thyme, parsley, basil, barley, salt, and pepper. Raise the heat to medium; stir well. Cover the kettle and let the soup come to a boil.

3. Let it boil for about 10 minutes. Then lower heat to low-medium, cover the kettle with the lid, and let the soup gently simmer for 20 to 30 minutes, until the soup is done. If the soup is very thick, add a bit more water. Serve the soup hot and top each serving with fresh parsley as garnish.

Saint Odo was one of the great medieval abbots of the monastery of Cluny, where he instigated many monastic reforms. His feast is celebrated in the monastic order on May 11. He is a patron of music.

MAIN
DISHES

ASPARAGUS WITH GARLIC SAUCE
ASPERGES SAUCE AÏOLI

6–8 servings

For the asparagus:
   1 lb medium-sized asparagus (Choose thinner stalks)
   6–8 hard-boiled eggs
   salt to taste

For the Sauce Aïoli (Garlic Mayonnaise):
   4 garlic cloves, peeled and crushed
   2 egg yolks
   1 Tbsp lemon juice or white wine
   1 Tbsp Dijon mustard
   1 1/2 cups olive oil
   salt to taste

1. Prepare the Sauce Aïoli. Place the finely crushed garlic, egg yolks, lemon juice, mustard, and salt in a deep bowl. Blend slowly with a mixer. Slowly add the oil, drop by drop, until the mixture thickens to the consistency of mayonnaise. Refrigerate the aïoli before using it.

2. Wash and trim the asparagus. Bring the water to boil in a large kettle. Add some salt. Then place the asparagus in the water and boil, covered, for about 8 minutes. Then uncover the kettle and simmer for another 5 minutes. The asparagus tips should be tender while the stalks remain firm. Rinse the asparagus in cold water.

3. Place 6 to 8 asparagus on each plate. Cut the hard-boiled eggs in four, lengthwise, and place them decoratively on top of the asparagus or to their side. Pour about four large spoons of the aïoli sauce over the center of the asparagus on each plate. Serve at room temperature.

The aïoli sauce is a traditional mayonnaise sauce from Provence. The Provençals love for garlic is well manifested in their unsparing use of it in most of their native dishes, and particularly in this delightful, pungent mayonnaise.

LETTUCE BREAD FROM THE DAUPHINE
PAIN DE LAITUE DAUPHINOIS

6 servings

6 eggs
1 cup heavy cream
salt and pepper to taste
freshly ground nutmeg
4 Tbsps flour
1 lb Boston lettuce leaves
butter

1. In a large bowl mix the eggs, heavy cream, salt and pepper, and a pinch of nutmeg. Using an electric mixer, beat the mixture thoroughly, while adding the flour a little bit at a time.

2. Separate the lettuce leaves. Wash them carefully and drain them thoroughly, seeing that no water remains on the leaves. Cut coarsely and add them to the mixture in the bowl, stirring it by hand.

3. Generously butter a bread pan, preferably one made of terra-cotta, and pour the mixture into it. Bake at 350° F for 45 minutes. Be careful that it does not overcook. Towards the end of the cooking time, place a thin knife into the bread to see if it is well done (the knife should come out clean). Let it cool before you take it from the mold. Place it on a flat serving dish and, if you wish to make it more attractive, place sliced tomatoes all around the bread.

It is a simple, light, and very appetizing dish from the Dauphine, one of the charming southeastern regions of France, which became incorporated into the rest of France in 1349. It is an ideal dish for an appetizer, or for a Sunday brunch.

> *Lead us, youthful shepherd, Holy One, King of souls,*
> *Lead us in your heavenly ways, O Word everlasting,*
> *Lead us, master of time, eternal light, and fountain of mercy!*
> ATTRIBUTED TO SAINT CLEMENT OF ALEXANDRIA

Scallops in Breadcrumbs
Coquilles Saint-Jacques à la Bretonne

6 servings

24 sea scallops
4 Tbsps butter
3 onions, chopped
3 shallots, chopped
1/2 cup breadcrumbs
1 cup Muscadet white wine
3 Tbsps chopped fresh parsley
salt and pepper to taste

1. Place the scallops in a large saucepan with boiling water to cover. Allow them to boil until the shells begin to open. Drain the shells in cold water and remove the scallops one by one, watching carefully to remove every bit of shell. Wash and drain the scallops, and chop them into small pieces.

2. Melt 3 tablespoons of butter in a large skillet, and when hot, add the chopped scallops, onions, and shallots. Sauté quickly for about 2 to 3 minutes. Add the white wine and chopped parsley. Gently mix in the breadcrumbs while stirring all the time. Cover the pan and simmer for at least 2 minutes.

3. Remove the skillet from the heat, add 1 tablespoon of butter to the mixture, and stir well. Butter thoroughly a flat baking dish, and spoon the scallop mixture into it. Sprinkle additional breadcrumbs on the top and a few drops of melted butter. Bake in a hot oven at 450° F for about 4 to 5 minutes. Serve hot.

The scallop is known in France as the pilgrim shell—a name derived from the fact that it was found in great numbers on the Galician coast of Spain, and their shells were used as emblems for pilgrims to the shrine of Saint James at Santiago de Compostella.

The aim of the contemplative life is not merely to enable a man to say prayers and make sacrifices with a right intention: it is to teach him to live in God.

THOMAS MERTON

ITALIAN FRITTATA
FRITATA À L'ITALIENNE

6 servings

1/4 cup olive
1 large onion, chopped
4 cooked potatoes, thinly diced (previously boiled)
8 eggs
salt and pepper to taste
1/2 cup chopped parsley

1. Pour olive oil into a large skillet and sauté the onion until golden. Add the boiled potatoes and stir for a few minutes.

2. Beat the eggs in a large bowl, adding the salt, pepper, and parsley. Stir well; pour the mixture over the vegetables in the skillet. Cook without stirring until the underside of the frittata is set.

3. Place skillet with the frittata under the broiler for a few minutes so that the top gets evenly cooked and brown. When the frittata is done, invert the skillet onto a platter, and serve hot.

The Italian frittata is the equivalent of the tortilla *española* (Spanish omelette) or the French omelette. It is a hearty dish that can be served either at lunch or supper. Often in some monasteries, especially on fast days, the monks would have some soup, an omelette, and a piece of fruit for their evening meal.

God bless the Ground! I shall walk softly there
And learn by going where I have to go.

THEODORE ROETHKE
THE WAKING

LENTILS WITH BROWN RICE
LENTILLES AU RIZ

4 servings

1 cup dried lentils, brown or green
1 cup mushrooms
1 medium-sized onion
6 garlic cloves
6 cups water
1 cup brown rice
6 Tbsps olive oil
1 tsp dried thyme
salt and pepper to taste
black olives (optional)

1. Wash and rinse the lentils.

2. Wash and rinse the mushrooms. Slice them thinly.

3. Slice and mince the onion and garlic cloves.

4. Place all the above in a large saucepan. Add the water, rice, olive oil, thyme, salt, and pepper.

5. Cover the saucepan, bringing its contents to a light boil. Reduce to medium-high heat, stirring from time to time so the contents do not stick to the bottom. When all the water has been absorbed, the dish is ready to be served. If you wish, garnish with black olives and serve with a green salad.

This combination of lentils and rice is called in French *repas complet* for it is a complete meal in itself, providing the total amount of protein one needs in a meal.

Historical evidence would indicate that very few inventions have been made by men who had to spend all their energy overcoming the immediate pressures of survival. The first genetic experiments, which led a hundred years later to high-yield agricultural crops took place in the peace of a European monastery.

DONELLA H. MEADOWS
LIMITS TO GROWTH

Spaghetti With Roquefort Cheese

SPAGHETTI AU ROQUEFORT

4 servings

3 qts water
1/4 lb spaghetti
4 ozs Roquefort cheese
4 ozs of crème fraîche (see page 213)
1 cup marsala wine
white pepper and salt to taste
chopped parsley, thin sliced walnuts as garnish

1. Pour about 3 quarts of water into a large pot and bring to a boil. Add the spaghetti, stirring so the pasta is totally immersed in the water. Add salt and cook the pasta for about 9 to 10 minutes, stirring from time to time.

2. While the spaghetti is boiling, finely chop half the Roquefort cheese and mix thoroughly with the crème fraîche. Add the marsala wine and the white pepper and continue mixing. Pour this mixture into a saucepan and cook rapidly over medium heat, while stirring continuously.

3. Drain the pasta and place in a serving bowl. Pour the sauce over it and mix well. Garnish the top with the chopped parsley, the sliced walnuts, and the rest of the Roquefort (crumbled). Serve hot.

This simple and rather original recipe provides one more variation of the different ways of preparing spaghetti. If there is no marsala around the house, one can substitute port wine or something similar. Steamed broccoli may be added to this dish as a variation.

*After silence that which
comes nearest to expressing
the inexpressible is music.*
        ALDOUS HUXLEY

FLEMISH EGGS
OEUFS À LA FLAMANDE

4 servings

> **1 large onion**
> **3 garlic cloves**
> **4 Tbsps olive oil**
> **1 red sweet pepper**
> **2 lbs frozen sweet peas (or canned peas)**
> **4 eggs**
> **paprika**
> **salt**

1. Peel the onion and garlic and slice and mince them well. In a large skillet sauté them in olive oil 2 to 3 minutes. Cut the pepper in thin long slices and add to the skillet. Continue sautéing for 3 more minutes.

2. Boil the frozen peas for about 3 minutes, or until tender. Rinse them thoroughly and gently pour the peas over the sautéed vegetables. Add salt and mix carefully.

3. Grease adequately either a large round dish of some depth or, preferably, four ceramic bowls for individual servings. Spread the vegetables in the dish, making a small cavity in the center for each egg. Crack open each egg delicately so the yolk stays whole and place an egg in each cavity and bake in the oven at 300° F until the egg whites achieve a solid consistency. Sprinkle with paprika and salt. Serve hot.

An uncomplicated dish to prepare, perfectly suitable for either a Sunday brunch or a light supper. In European monasteries it is often served on Sundays or feast days.

> *I never ask God to give himself to me, I beg of him to purify, to empty me. If I am empty, God of his very nature is obliged to give himself to me to fill me.*
>
> MEISTER ECKHART

Sorrel au Gratin
Oseille au Gratin

4 servings

> **2 cups water**
> **10 cups thinly cut sorrel (or spinach)**
> **3 to 4 Tbsps olive oil**
> **1 medium-sized onion, thinly sliced**
> **1 cup of Béchamel sauce (see page 206)**
> **2 egg yolks, beaten**
> **1/3 cup grated cheese (Cheddar, Romano, or Gruyère)**

1. In a large stainless steel saucepan bring the water to a boil. Add the sorrel and let it boil for no more than 2 or 3 minutes. Drain the sorrel thoroughly.

2. Pour the oil into a skillet and sauté the sliced onion over medium heat for about 2 minutes until it begins to turn golden.

3. Prepare the Béchamel sauce. Beat the egg yolks and add to the Béchamel sauce. Blend thoroughly. Then add the well-drained sorrel and the onion, and blend the mixture very well.

4. Pour the mixture into a well-buttered flat baking dish and sprinkle some grated cheese of your preference over the entire surface. Bake in a preheated oven at 350° F for about 15 minutes. The gratin is ready when it has turned into an even, thick consistency. Serve hot.

Sorrel, with its particular sour flavor, is one of those rather popular and favorite vegetables throughout France. It is often used in simple home and monastic kitchens, as well as by the chefs of the *haute cuisine française*. Again, there are endless ways of preparing this delicious vegetable. This recipe is rather simple and basic, one that would be pleasing to most people.

Prayer looks out all the time towards God and stretches towards God with desire. Jeremy Taylor describes it wonderfully when he says: "Prayer is only the body of the soul. Desires are its wings!"

EVELYN UNDERHILL

PARSLEY POTATOES
POMMES PERSILLÉES

6 servings

> **1 1/2 pounds medium-sized new potatoes**
> **6 Tbsps olive or other vegetable oil**
> **2 tsps butter or margarine, melted**
> **1/2 cup fresh parsley, minced**
> **salt and pepper to taste**

1. Wash and peel the potatoes. Rinse them in cold water and drain them thoroughly. Pour some water in a large saucepan. The water should be at least 3" to 4" deep. Place the potatoes either in a double boiler or a steamer basket over the water and cook over medium heat for about 20 to 30 minutes. Neither the double boiler nor the basket should touch the water.

2. When the potatoes are ready, pour the oil and melted butter into a large saucepan. Turn off the heat and, immediately, add the finely chopped parsley, salt and pepper, and the potatoes. Cover the pan and gently shake it. Make sure that the potatoes are thoroughly coated with the oil and parsley. Leave the saucepan covered until you are ready to serve and again gently shake once more before serving. Serve hot.

This is a very popular way of preparing potatoes throughout France. This preparation makes a lovely accompaniment to a soufflé or to other egg or fish dishes.

The very best and utmost of attainment in life
is to remain still and let God act and speak in thee.

MEISTER ECKHART

LENTILS AU GRATIN
GRATIN DE LENTILLES

4-6 servings

6 Tbsps olive oil
2 onions, chopped
1 carrot, thinly sliced
1 celery stalk, thinly sliced
2 cups brown lentils
3 garlic cloves, minced
salt and pepper to taste
5 cups water
3 eggs
1/3 cup milk
1/3 cup breadcrumbs
1/2 cup grated cheddar cheese
4 Tbsps mixed herbs (parsley, thyme, oregano)

1. Pour the oil into a large saucepan, add the onion, carrot, and celery; sauté them for about 2 minutes. Add the lentils, garlic, salt and pepper, and water, and allow it to boil for about 25 to 30 minutes over medium heat. Stir from time to time. When the lentils are cooked, if some water remains, drain them in a colander.

2. Beat the eggs in a bowl. Add the milk and beat some more. Add the breadcrumbs, 1/4 cup cheese, and mixed herbs, and mix very well. Add the cooked lentils and vegetables and mix thoroughly.

3. Butter a flat baking dish and pour the mixture into it. Using a spatula, smooth the surface of the mixture. Sprinkle the remaining grated cheese on top. Bake at 350° F for 40 minutes. Serve hot during the cold months or refrigerate and serve cold during the warm weather.

And like the fish, swimming in the vast sea and resting in its deeps, and like the bird boldly mounting high in the sky, so the soul feels its spirit freely moving through the vastness and the depth and the unutterable richnesses of love.

BEATRICE OF NAZARETH
TWELFTH-CENTURY BEGUINE

POLENTA BASQUE STYLE
POLENTA À LA BASQUAISE

4 servings

For the polenta:
- 1 cup milk
- 1 1/2 cups cornmeal
- 3 1/2 cups water
- 1 large onion, chopped
- 3 Tbsps vegetable oil
- 1 tsp salt
- 1 cup grated Parmesan cheese
- 4 Tbsps butter

For the sauce:
- 1 large onion
- 1 green bell pepper
- 1 red bell pepper
- 2 medium-sized zucchini
- parsley
- salt to taste
- 6 to 8 Tbsps vegetable oil

1. The easiest way to prepare the polenta without burning it is to use a double boiler. Pour the milk in the top of the double boiler with the water already boiling, add the cornmeal slowly, stirring continually.

2. In a separate pan bring the water to a boil. Pour the boiling water into the cornmeal mixture, stirring continually. Cook over a very low flame, stirring constantly, until the mixture comes to a boil.

3. Sauté the onion in vegetable oil. Then add the salt, cheese, and onion to the double boiler and mix the entire thing very well.

4. Butter a long baking dish (8" x 12") and pour the cornmeal mixture into it, adding butter on top, and sprinkling some grated cheese over the top of the polenta. Bake at 300° F for about 30 minutes, until the top turns golden.

5. In a large frying pan, sauté the thinly sliced onions, peppers, and zucchini in vegetable oil until they begin to turn slightly brown. Add a pinch of salt and the well-minced parsley. Stir and serve as a sauce on top of the polenta. (After it comes out of the oven, the polenta can be sliced in square pieces and served as such at the table, spreading a good bit of sauce on top.)

Polenta is a thoroughly nutritious meal that can be served hot during the cold days or cold during the warm weather.

BROCCOLI AND POTATOES GRATIN
GRATIN DE BROCOLI ET POMMES DE TERRE

6 servings

3 large heads broccoli
6 medium-sized potatoes, peeled
6 garlic cloves, well minced
1 pint heavy cream
1/4 tsp freshly grated nutmeg
salt and pepper to taste
olive oil
1/2 cup grated mozzarella cheese, to cover top of dish

1. Cook the broccoli and the potatoes separately in boiling water until they are soft and tender. Drain and chop them coarsely.

2. Place the broccoli and the potatoes in a deep bowl, add the minced garlic, heavy cream, nutmeg, salt and pepper to taste. Mix very well.

3. With olive oil, grease thoroughly a long flat dish and generously sprinkle grated cheese over its entire surface. Closely pack the vegetable mixture into the greased dish and smooth evenly. Cover the entire top with grated cheese and bake in the oven at 350° F for about 30 minutes. Serve hot.

The Christian life is a journey....Therefore do not wait for great strength before setting out, for immobility will weaken you further. Do not wait to see very clearly before starting: one has to walk toward the light.

THE CHOICE IS ALWAYS OURS
DOROTHY BERKLEY PHILIPS, EDITOR

CRÊPES WITH SPINACH FILLING
CRÊPES AUX EPINARDS

6 servings

For the crêpes:
- 4 eggs
- 2 Tbsps vegetable oil
- 1 1/4 cups all-purpose flour
- pinch of salt
- 4 cups whole milk
- 1/2 pint heavy cream

For the filling:
- butter
- 1 onion, chopped
- 1 lb fresh spinach, cooked and chopped
- 4 hard-boiled eggs, chopped
- 1 cup grated Gruyère cheese
- salt and pepper to taste

1. In a large bowl, mix the eggs, oil, flour, and salt and beat with a mixer, adding one cup of milk at a time. The batter must have the consistency of heavy cream and should be free of flour lumps. If the batter is too thick, add one or two teaspoons of cold water and continue to mix until it is light and smooth. Refrigerate the batter for an hour or two before starting to use.

2. Heat a 6" or 8" crêpe skillet over a high flame and lightly grease the entire skillet with a bit of oil or melted butter using a small pastry brush. Using a small ladle, pour the batter into the skillet. Tip it immediately so the batter covers the entire bottom of the skillet and quickly becomes firm. Cook the crêpe for about 1 minute, until it begins to show signs of turning brown around the rim. Turn it over rapidly with a spatula and cook the reverse side for another minute. When the crêpe is done, slide it gently onto a flat plate. Brush the skillet once more with oil or butter and continue as before until all the crêpes are cooked.

3. In a nonaluminum pan, melt the butter and gently sauté the onion. Add the already boiled and chopped spinach. Cook for a minute or two. Turn heat off. Add the chopped hard-boiled eggs, grated cheese, salt, and pepper. Blend everything well.

4. Generously butter a large baking dish. Fill each crêpe with the spinach mixture, roll it up, and place it carefully in the baking dish, one next to the other. When all the crêpes are in the pan, cover them with heavy cream and bake them at 300° F for about 15 to 20 minutes. Serve them hot.

he spinach may be easily replaced with sorrel or Swiss chard.

GREEN RICE
RIZ VERT

6 servings

4 Tbsps olive oil
1 large onion, well chopped
2 cups long-grain rice
1 cup well-chopped sorrel (or spinach)
4 1/2 cups water
salt and pepper to taste

1. Pour the olive oil into a deep saucepan and sauté the onion and the rice for 2 to 3 minutes, until they begin to brown. Stir continually.

2. Pass the sorrel with 2 cups of water through a blender until thoroughly blended. Pour this into the rice, add the remaining water, and a pinch of salt and pepper. Stir well and cook slowly over low heat until all the liquid is absorbed. Serve hot.

All men cannot be monks:
we have different paths allotted to us
to mount to the high seat of eternal felicity.

CERVANTES

DEVILED EGGS WITH SARDINES
OEUFS AUX SARDINES

6 servings

6 hard-boiled eggs
2-oz can sardines
5 Tbsps mayonnaise
1 Tbsp lemon juice
1 tsp Dijon mustard
a few sprigs of parsley, thinly cut and well minced
salt and white pepper to taste

1. Cut the hard-boiled eggs in half lengthwise. Carefully take out the yolks and place them in a bowl. Be careful that the whites of the eggs remain firm and intact.

2. Slice the sardines into tiny pieces and place them in the bowl with the egg yolks. Mash together thoroughly with a strong fork. Add the mayonnaise, lemon juice, mustard, minced parsley, salt, and pepper; and mix well.

3. Fill the egg whites with the mixture, place them in a dish, cover them with foil, and keep refrigerated until they are ready to be served.

This simple and appetizing dish can be used for lunch, brunch, or as an elegant hors d'oeuvre for a dinner party. The eggs can be accompanied by slices of ripe tomatoes and black olives. And, of course, slices of fresh French bread!

*In the evening of life
we shall be judged on love.*
SAINT JOHN OF THE CROSS

SORREL OMELET
OMELETTE À L'OSEILLE

2 servings

> 1/3 cup white sauce (see page 207)
> 1 cup sorrel, well chopped
> 6 Tbsps butter
> 5 eggs
> 2 Tbsps water or milk
> salt and pepper to taste
> 1/3 cup grated Gruyère cheese (optional)

1. Prepare white sauce.

2. In an omelet skillet, sauté the chopped sorrel in 3 tablespoons butter for about 3 to 4 minutes. Blend thoroughly with the white sauce. Set aside.

3. Beat the eggs in a bowl, counting at least 20 brisk strokes. Add the milk, salt and pepper, and continue beating the egg mixture until it all blends.

4. Melt the remaining 3 tablespoons of butter in the skillet, run it all over the pan and let it get bubbly hot without burning. Pour in the egg mixture rapidly before the butter begins to turn brown. Spread the eggs evenly around the pan using a spatula. When the egg mixture sets firmly on the bottom, turn the omelet by placing a dish over it and turning quickly. Gently slide the reverse side of the omelet back onto the skillet, pour the sorrel mixture and the cheese, if desired, in the center, and allow it to cook for about 2 minutes. Fold one half of the omelet carefully over the other half. Slice the omelet in half and serve immediately on warm plates.

Though most people in France would prefer the taste of sorrel to that of spinach or Swiss chard for this particular omelet, these can easily be substituted for sorrel in the regions or areas where sorrel is not cultivated. In that case, both the spinach and the chard should be boiled first and thoroughly drained before mixing with the white sauce.

The earth has enough for every man's need but not for every man's greed.

MAHATMA GANDHI

Minty Peas With Small Onions

PETITS POIS ET OIGNIONS A LA MENTHE

6 servings

2 cups fresh or frozen peas
10-oz package frozen small onions
3 branches fresh mint
salt to taste
a few mint leaves, thinly sliced and minced
2 Tbsps butter
freshly ground pepper to taste

1. Place the peas, onions, and mint branches in a good-sized casserole filled with water. Boil them over medium-high heat for about 8 to 10 minutes, until tender. Drain them and discard the mint branches.

2. Melt the butter in a saucepan, add the peas and onions, mint leaves, and pepper. Stir constantly over low-medium heat until all ingredients are well blended. Serve at once, as an accompaniment to the main course.

Singing is not worth a thing if the heart sings not the song,
and the heart can never sing if it brings not love along.

HARVEY BIRENBAUM

SALADS

Saint Joseph's Salad
SALADE SAINT-JOSEPH

6 servings

1 lb fresh asparagus
1 lb fresh white mushrooms
12 ozs artichoke hearts (canned or frozen)
4 medium-sized endives
minced parsley
simple vinaigrette with lemon juice (see page 214)

1. Wash and rinse the asparagus. Cut them in small pieces about 2 inches long. Bring the water to boil in a large saucepan. Place the asparagus in a deep colander and plunge the asparagus into the boiling water for 4 to 5 minutes. Rinse them at once in cold water and drain them well.

2. Wash and rinse the mushrooms. Cut them into thin slices. Wash and drain the endive. Cut the leaves in half lengthwise.

3. Put the endives, mushrooms, asparagus, and artichoke hearts into a deep salad bowl. Sprinkle the finely minced parsley over the vegetables.

4. Prepare a simple vinaigrette (substitute the lemon juice for the vinegar) and pour over the salad just before serving. Toss the salad and serve.

Saint Joseph's feasts are celebrated on March 19 and on May 1. He certainly can be considered a spring saint and though this wonderful salad may be enjoyed all year round, it is most appropriate to have in early spring when asparagus is in season.

SPINACH SALAD
SALADE D'EPINARDS

4 servings

1 bunch fresh spinach (enough to serve 4)
4 hard-boiled eggs
1 medium-sized red onion
vinaigrette (see page 214)

1. Wash and rinse the spinach thoroughly.

2. Hard-boil the eggs, then rinse them in cold water, and peel and slice them evenly. Cut the onion in round, thin slices and place them in a bowl of hot water for about 3 minutes. This takes the sting away, but not the taste. Rinse thoroughly in cold water. Drain it.

3. Place the spinach, onion, and eggs in a large bowl. Prepare the vinaigrette, and pour it over the salad just before serving. Mix well.

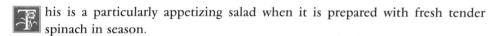 his is a particularly appetizing salad when it is prepared with fresh tender spinach in season.

SPRING SALAD

SALADE PRINTANIERE

4-6 servings

1 large head leaf lettuce (or 2 small heads of Boston lettuce)
12 cherry tomatoes
4 hard-boiled eggs
5 Tbsps olive oil
2 Tbsps lemon juice
salt and pepper to taste

1. Wash and rinse thoroughly the lettuce and tomatoes. The tomatoes should be dried with a paper towel and cut in quarters.

2. Peel the eggs and cut them also in four quarters.

3. Prepare a vinaigrette by mixing the olive oil, lemon juice, salt, and pepper.

4. On a large salad plate, first place the lettuce leaves, then add the tomatoes and the hard-boiled eggs. Just before serving, stir the vinaigrette once more and pour gently over the salad.

*The riches that are in the heart
can not be stolen.*

RUSSIAN PROVERB

RED SALAD
SALADE ROUGE

4-6 servings

1 lb cherry tomatoes
1 lb fresh radishes
1 large red onion
a few sprigs of parsley

1. Wash and rinse well the tomatoes and the radishes. Trim them and then slice them in perfect halves lengthwise.

2. Slice the red onion in thin, even slices and place in a bowl of slightly hot water for about 10 minutes. This will take its sting away. Rinse thoroughly with cold water. Place the tomatoes, radishes, and onion in a large mixing bowl.

3. Prepare a homemade vinaigrette or mayonnaise, or use one commercially made if you prefer. Pour it over the vegetables and mix well. Before serving, sprinkle some fresh chopped parsley over the entire salad.

o serve this salad cold, refrigerate before serving. But the vinaigrette or mayonnaise sauce should be added immediately before serving.

Every single creature is full of God and is a book about God. Every creature is a word about God. If I spent enough time with the tiniest creature—even a caterpillar—I would never have to prepare a sermon, so full of God is every creature.

MEISTER ECKHART

Spring, the sweet spring, is the years pleasant king;
Then blooms each thing, then maids dance in a ring.
Cold doth not sting, the pretty birds do sing.
Cuckoo, jug, jug, pu we, to witta woo.
The fields breathe sweet, the daisies kiss our feet,
Young lovers meet, old wives a-sunning sit,
In every street these tunes our ears do greet,
Cuckoo, jug, jug, pu we, to witta woo.

THOMAS NASHE

DESSERTS

SNOWY EGGS
OEUFS À LA NEIGE

6 servings

6 egg whites
1/2 cup sugar
1 vanilla bean
4 cups milk
2 Tbsps water
English Cream (page 42)

1. Place a vanilla bean in 1/2 cup sugar and stir it around so the flavor of the bean goes through the sugar. Remove the bean for use later in the boiling milk. Beat the egg whites into a stiff meringue, adding little by little the sugar which was mixed with the vanilla bean.

2. Pour the milk into a saucepan and bring to boil. Add the vanilla bean. With a large tablespoon, scoop out a ball of the meringue and place it gently into the scalded milk, poach one side of the "snow ball" for about 2 minutes. Gently turn and poach the other side for the same amount of time. When they are done, gently withdraw the "snow balls" one by one with a spoon, and place them over a clean kitchen towel. Allow them to cool. The milk can then be used to prepare the English Cream.

3. Prepare the English Cream (Crème Anglaise).

4. When the cream is ready, remove the vanilla bean, pour into a deep serving bowl or into 6 individual dessert bowls. Carefully place the "snow balls" over the cream and allow them to float. Chill the dessert in the refrigerator for a few hours before serving.

This is a very old traditional dessert throughout France, and both children and grownups love it. Some people prefer poaching the meringue balls in boiling water and swear they come out more beautiful. However, I suggest using milk in this recipe simply because of the practicality of using the milk later to prepare the Crème Anglaise.

PASTRY CREAM WITH PEACHES

CREME PATISSIÈRE AUX PÊCHES

6 servings

12-oz can sliced peaches, drained
6 egg whites, beaten stiff
2 Tbsps sugar
1 tsp vanilla extract
English Cream (See page 42)

1. Prepare the English cream.

2. Pour the cream into a long flat baking dish and arrange the sliced peaches on the top in such a way as to cover the entire surface.

3. Prepare a meringue by mixing the egg whites, vanilla, and sugar, and beating them until stiff. Cover the peaches with the meringue.

4. Place the dish in the oven and bake at 350° F for 15 minutes or at least until the meringue turns to a golden brown color. Refrigerate and serve cold.

I know not what I shall become: it seems to me that peace of soul and repose of spirit descend on me even in sleep. I only know that God keeps me. I am in a calm so great that I fear nought. What can I fear, when I am with God?

BROTHER LAWRENCE

APPLE TART
TARTE AUX POMMES

6 servings

For the filling:
   5 apples
   2 Tbsps lemon juice
   1/3 cup sugar

For the custard mix:
   2 egg yolks
   3 Tbsps sugar
   1/2 cup heavy cream
   1 Tbsp Calvados

**For the pastry shell
(la Pâté Brisée):**
   1 egg
   1 cup flour
   1 stick sweet butter
   5 Tbsps ice water
   pinch of salt

1. Wash, peel, and core the apples. Cut the apples in fine slices, place them in a bowl and add the lemon juice and sugar. Mix gently and set the bowl aside.

2. Prepare the pastry shell by mixing all the ingredients in a good-sized bowl. Use a fork and your hands for mixing until the dough is made. Do not overwork. Form a ball with the dough and sprinkle flour all around it. Place the dough in the refrigerator and let it rest for 1 hour.

3. When the dough is ready to be worked, sprinkle sufficient flour over the table or a large board and carefully roll the dough out, extending it in every direction. Thoroughly butter a tart or pie dish and place the rolled dough into it with care. The dough must always be handled with the fingers. Trim the edges, forming a decorative design. Cover the pastry shell with aluminum foil and place in the oven at 250° F and prebake for about 12 to 15 minutes.

4. Remove the pastry shell from the oven and fill with at least two even apple layers following the design of a revolving wheel. Sprinkle some sugar on top and bake at 350° F for about 20 minutes.

5. Prepare the custard mixture by blending all the ingredients in a bowl with an electric mixer. When the pie crust begins to turn brown and the apples seem baked, pour the custard mixture evenly over the entire surface. Continue baking for another 12 minutes or so until the custard appears bubbly and brown on top. Let it cool before serving.

CHOCOLATE BÉCHAMEL CREAM
BÉCHAMEL AU CHOCOLAT

4 servings

3 cups milk
5 ozs chocolate
1/2 cup granulated sugar
4 Tbsps butter
4 Tbsps cornstarch

1. Scald the milk and dissolve the chocolate and sugar in it.

2. Melt the butter in a saucepan. Add the flour and stir continuously for 2 or 3 minutes. Slowly pour the chocolate milk into the butter-flour mixture, stirring constantly. Cook slowly over medium-low heat while continuing to stir for about 10 minutes. Bring to a boiling point and turn off the heat. Refrigerate and serve cold.

A misty winter, frosty spring,
a varied summer and a sunny harvest:
an ideal year.

IRISH PROVERB

PEARS FLAMBÉ
POIRES FLAMBÉES

6 servings

9 pears, not overly ripe
1 cup water
3/4 cup granulated sugar
2 tsps lemon juice
raspberry liqueur or pear liqueur

1. Peel the pears. Cut them in half and scoop out the seeds.

2. Pour the water and sugar into a spacious saucepan and slowly, over low heat, begin to make a syrup. Place the pears in the syrup, add the lemon juice, and cook them for a few minutes, turning them over at least once. Place the pears carefully in a compote bowl and refrigerate for hour.

3. Place 3 pear halves in each serving dish, pour some raspberry liqueur (or another one of your preference) on the top, and flambé them at the table.

EGG CUSTARD
OEUFS AU LAIT

6 servings

1 qt milk
5 ozs sugar
1 Tbsp vanilla extract or rum
1 slice of lemon peel
5 eggs

1. Pour the milk into a saucepan, add the sugar, vanilla extract, and lemon peel. Bring to a boil.

2. In a large bowl, thoroughly beat the eggs with a mixer. Add the boiled milk slowly, pouring a little at a time while continuing to mix. Discard the lemon peel.

3. Pour the contents into six small ramekins (individual custard dishes). Place them into a long ovenproof dish, or similar container, filled with water to cook *au bain-marie*. Place it in the oven and cook at 350° F for about 30 to 35 minutes. Take it from the oven and let it cool. Serve cold.

VENETIAN CREAM
CRÈME VÉNITIENNE

4-6 servings

English Cream (page 42)
6 egg whites

1. Prepare a basic English Cream. Do not allow it to cool.

2. With an electric mixer, beat the egg whites separately until they turn firm. Pour the stiffened egg whites slowly into the English Cream while the cream is still warm. Fold and mix well with the help of a fork. This delicious cream can be served while hot or refrigerate and serve cold.

O God, you are the light of the minds that know you, the life of the souls that love you, and the strength of the wills that serve you; help us so to know you that we may truly love you, so to love you that we may fully serve you.

SAINT AUGUSTINE

Lemon Soufflé
Soufflé au Citron

4 servings

1/2 granulated cup sugar (add more if desired)
2 Tbsps butter
2 Tbsps cornstarch (or flour)
2 tsps lemon juice and one slice lemon rind
1 cup whole milk
3 egg yolks, well beaten
1 tsp pure vanilla extract
3 egg whites, well beaten

1. In a large bowl, place the sugar, butter, cornstarch, lemon juice, and rind. Mix it well with an electric mixer until creamy. Add the milk, egg yolks, and vanilla, and mix thoroughly. Then fold in the egg whites, which have been well beaten.

2. Pour the mixture into four small well-buttered ramekins (individual custard dishes) and set them in a shallow pan containing water. Bake at 300° F for about 20 minutes or until the top turns brown and fluffy. To check whether the soufflé is perfectly baked, simply insert a long clean needle into it. When the needle comes out clean, the soufflé is done. The soufflé must be served quickly, while the head is still up.

his is a straight and uncomplicated way of preparing a lemon soufflé for dessert on a day when one doesn't wish to fuss with difficult preparations and yet would like to present something special at the table. It is a rather quick and simple recipe.

God is wise, and loves you with wisdom,
God is good, and loves you with goodness,
God is holy, and loves you with holiness,
God is just, and loves you with justice,
God is merciful, and loves you with mercy,
God is compassionate and understanding, and loves
you with gentleness and sweetness.

SAINT JOHN OF THE CROSS

Pear Clafoutis
Clafoutis aux Poires

6-8 servings

4 ripe pears
1 cup whole milk
3 eggs
1/2 cup granulated sugar
2 Tbsps cognac (or vanilla if desired)
confectioners' sugar

1. Preheat oven to 350° F.

2. Peel and slice the pears.

3. To prepare the batter, place the milk, eggs, sugar, and cognac in the blender and whirl them thoroughly at high speed for a minute or two.

4. Generously butter a square baking dish about 1" to 2" deep. Pour about one-fourth of the batter into the baking dish and place in the oven for about 2 minutes until the batter has set in the bottom of the dish. Remove from the oven and spread the sliced pears evenly over the surface of the batter. (At this point, if one wishes, one can sprinkle a bit of sugar over the fruit.) Pour the rest of the batter on top of the fruit, smoothing evenly. Place in the center of the oven and bake for about 40 minutes. The clafouti is done when the top puffs and turns brown, though still remaining custard-like. Remove from the oven, sprinkle some confectioners' sugar on top and serve at the table while the clafouti is still warm.

The clafouti is a traditional dessert that claims to be originally from the central part of France, yet it is so well known and popular throughout the whole of France that each region possesses its own version. Though traditionally made with cherries, one can easily substitute any fruit that is in season.

The most uncompromising farmer is God Himself.

CARLO CARETTO
LETTERS FROM THE DESERT

OLD-FASHIONED BREAD PUDDING
PUDDING À L'ANCIENNE

4-6 servings

1 1/4 cups granulated sugar
4 cups scalded milk
2 cups stale breadcrumbs (any day-old bread will do)
1 cup dried seedless raisins
2 eggs
1/2 tsp salt
1 tsp vanilla extract
1 tsp brandy
heavy cream

1. In a medium-sized pan, caramelize 1/2 cup of sugar until it becomes golden brown. Carefully add the scalded milk and stir until the caramel is dissolved.

2. Remove from heat. Add the breadcrumbs and raisins and let soak for about 20 to 25 minutes.

3. Using a mixer, whip together the two eggs, the remaining sugar, salt, vanilla, and brandy. Pour into the bread-raisin mixture. Stir all together and pour into a flat well-greased baking dish. Bake for about 1 hour at 325° F. As you serve it, pour some heavy cream on the top of each serving.

Texture was important in medieval eating because of the limited number of eating tools used. Most people carried a knife of the old, general purpose dagger shape, and spoons were not uncommon. But the dinner fork was an oddity in most of Europe until the eighteenth century.

REAY TANNAHILL
FOOD IN HISTORY

SUMMER

The summer days are come again;
Once more the glad earth yields
Her golden wealth of rip'ning grain;
And breath of clover fields,
And deepening shade of summer woods,
And glow of summer air....

SAMUEL LONGFELLOW

W hat is one to say about June?" wrote Gertrude Jekyll in the 1890s. "The time of perfect young summer, the fulfillment of the promise of the earlier months, and with as yet no sign to remind one that its fresh young beauty will ever fade. For my own part, I wander up into the woods and say, "June is here—June is here; thank God for lovely June!"

June is one of the most pleasant, most gentle months of the year. It is, perhaps, the gardener's favorite month if he or she were to choose one. The gradual warming up of the weather allows the flower beds, in particular, the eye-catching perennials, to display abundantly the magic of their colors. To the trained eye of the gardener, it is immensely satisfying to gaze at this profusion of colors with the clear-blue sky of June in the background; white and pink foxgloves, blue-purple lavender and lupines, white and pale-blue campanulas, orange-fire Oriental poppy, white daisies, bright yellow coreopsis, red astilbes, and, of course, roses of all colors and shades. This symphony of colors can be seen, not only in the well-ordered cultivated garden but also by the roadsides and in the nearby meadows. There are fields and fields covered with moon daisies, wild geraniums, phlox, and black-eyed Susans that are a true feast to the eyes.

Early summer is also a time when the first delicacies from the vegetable garden begin to arrive, sweet peas, tender spinach, lettuce, sweet onions, radishes, arugula, scallions, sorrel...and the local farmers begin to offer the first strawberries, blueberries, and blackberries of the season! It is sheer joy to roam around the back country roads looking for the wild counterparts of these berries. This is truly a glorious time for both cooks and gardeners...but also a time of tedious, intensive, and vigorous work: there is the weeding and hoeing, watering and endless care of the plants, pruning the dead flowers, and, of course, the grass cutting continues at a regular pace. There is no immediate relief in sight.

Summer begins officially on June 21, the time of the summer solstice, the longest day of the year. After this, the daylight begins to recede slowly. Early summer also brings to us the liturgical feast of Saint John the Baptist on June 24 and that of the apostles Saint Peter and Saint Paul on June 29. In primitive Europe, its inhabitants celebrated the summer solstice with enormous bonfires. When Europe was Christianized, however, this celebration was moved to the eve of Saint John the

Baptist's feast. That is, to June 23, a celebration that continues to this day, even in the most remote places of Europe. To this day it is a lovely experience to drive at sunset on June 23 through the old French country roads and see those grand old fires rising to the skies, with local village people talking, singing, and dancing around them.

As we move further into summer, in the midst of its sultry heat, we reach the Fourth of July, and we are glad to celebrate not only America's Independence Day, but particularly the values for which the country stands: freedom and democracy. And for us monks, the yearly solemnity of Saint Benedict arrives on July 11. Saint Benedict is the father of western monasticism and also the patron saint of Europe. His feast is celebrated with great joy in all monasteries. There are flowers in abundance in the chapel and refectory, and at the table we are presented with delicacies freshly harvested from the garden and orchards. July is a prolific month for fruits: currants, gooseberries, peaches, plums, apricots. These fruits, served alone or in a variety of ways (fruit salads, compotes, and sorbets), are the most healthy and rewarding way to end a summer meal.

As the season advances from July into August, some of the early perennials cease flowering and make room for late-blooming perennials: daylilies, hostas, shasta daisies, cornflowers, monkshoods, hollyhocks, summer jasmine. Midsummer is also the time when the annuals begin to show off in profusion: nasturtiums, zinnias, cosmos, marigolds, dahlias, blue salvia, snapdragons, and the royal sunflowers. Their colors add unusual beauty to the late summer garden, almost a hint of the approaching colors of the fall. The seasonal continuity of lush abundance shows at this time in the vegetable garden. The first tomatoes begin to ripen, and as all cooks know, there is nothing to compare to home-grown tomatoes! The fresh corn is harvested with the incomparable sweetness for which we wait all year long. Then there are the summer squash, zucchini, cucumbers, beans, and first potatoes, to say nothing of the basil and some of the fresh herbs that develop their most aromatic scent at this time. Fruits, like melons and peaches, are also harvested during the sunny and often humid month of August.

For cooks, the one setback can be that the kitchen itself, because of the intense heat, can become a less than desirable place to be at this time. The remedy for such nuisance is to rely more on salads of all sorts, cold soups, cheeses, yogurt, and plenty of fresh fruit.

The peak, liturgically speaking, of the summer monastic feasts is the Transfiguration of the Lord on August 6 and the Dormition of the Mother of God on August 15. The feast of the Transfiguration is truly a feast of the light, since it commemorates Jesus' appearance at Mount Tabor clothed in the divine light. Jesus appeared so luminous, so resplendent, to the disciples gazing at him that they became blinded by the light of God's glory shining in the face of their Master. For the monk as well as for the ordinary Christian, the feast of the Transfiguration is of particular meaning. We are all called to share in the mystery of the Transfiguration and to become inwardly transformed by the same divine light. In the Christian East, where this feast is celebrated with great solemnity, the faithful bring to church the first fruits and vegetables from their garden to be blessed during the liturgy. It is a symbol of the earth itself being made new by the presence of Christ and rendering in homage its first fruits to its Lord and Master.

On August 15, we gather again for another of our summer highlights. The Dormition of Our Lady is considered the most important of the feasts dedicated to Mary, the Mother of God. In the Christian East, the feast is preceded by a two-week fast. One of the Byzantine texts for the Vespers of the feast conveys beautifully the meaning of the feast: "The source of life is laid in the grave and her tomb becomes a ladder to heaven." The feast commemorates both the earthly death of the Virgin and her glorious Assumption into heaven. The Assumption is a feast not only of the Virgin but also of all human nature. For it is our redeemed human nature that is carried up and received with her into heaven.

Summer is a season of subtle changes, growth, and ultimately, transformation. The lush exuberance and intensity of summer living definitely influences the human experience: our innermost thoughts, our intuitions, our activities, our interaction with others, our relationship with our own selves and with God. Summer gives us a vivid sense of the reality of living and instigates the continuous discovery of what living is for.

When the summer days begin to wane and the summer moon drifts away, we are ready for moving into the next cycle, the quiet ripening of the seeds planted by the Spirit into the soil of our very lives. The words of Rowland Robinson come appropriately to mind: "Summer wanes, flowers fade, bird songs falter to mournful notes of farewell: but while regretfully we mark the decline of these golden days, we remember with a thrill of expectation that they slope to the golden days of autumn, wherein the farmer garners his latest harvest."

Teach this triple truth to all:
a generous heart, kind speech,
and a life of service and compassion
are the things which renew humanity.
BUDDHA

SOUPS AND APPETIZERS

CLUNY SALMON DIP
MOUSSE AU SAUMON DE CLUNY

makes a medium-sized bowl

2 lbs smoked salmon, thinly sliced
10 ozs cream cheese
5 ozs mayonnaise
8 ozs low-fat sour cream
4 Tbsps lemon juice
5 cornichons, cut in small pieces
2 scallions, finely sliced
2 flat-leaf parsley (Italian), finely chopped
black pepper to taste

1. Place all the above ingredients in a blender and mix thoroughly until an even, creamy mixture is achieved. Place the mixture into a serving bowl and keep it refrigerated until ready to serve.

2. When ready to serve, spread the mixture over crackers or thinly sliced bread (baguette)—and serve. (Or simply present the dip in the bowl, surrounded by crackers and thin bread slices.)

The monastery of Cluny in France was one of the great centers of monasticism during the Middle Ages.

ICED TOMATO SOUP
SOUPE FROIDE AUX TOMATOES

4-6 servings

1/3 cup olive oil
4 leeks (only the white parts), sliced
8 large tomatoes, peeled and sliced
8 cups water
bouquet garni
4 garlic cloves, minced
2 Tbsps lemon juice
1 Tbsp lime juice
pinch of sugar
salt and pepper to taste

1. Make the bouquet garni by tying together with a thin thread the leaves or sprigs of different herbs (bay leaf, thyme, basil leaves, parsley, and rosemary).

2. Pour the oil in a large saucepan, add the leeks and tomatoes, peeled and sliced in quarters. Sauté until the tomatoes dissolve into a sauce.

3. Add the water and the remaining ingredients. Cover and let boil over medium heat for about 30 minutes. Remove the bouquet garni and pass the soup through a strainer or a food mill and refrigerate for at least 4 hours. Serve very chilled.

 n ideal soup to serve on a hot summer day, especially during the midsummer and after, when fresh tomatoes begin to appear in the garden and the markets.

> *God, I can push the grass apart*
> *and lay my finger on Thy heart.*
> EDNA ST. VINCENT MILLAY
> *RENASCENCE*

LEMONY CARROT SOUP

SOUPE AUX CARROTTES

4-6 servings

8 large carrots
2 onions
1 1/2 cups whole milk
2 Tbsps flour
6 Tbsps olive oil
pinch of dried or fresh thyme
salt and pepper to taste
3 tsps lemon juice
finely minced fresh parsley

1. Wash and peel the carrots and onions. Chop them fairly fine. Place them in a soup pot with twice as much the amount of water as vegetables. Cook slowly until it boils, then let it simmer for 20 minutes.

2. Add the milk, flour, oil, thyme, salt, and pepper. Pass the whole thing through the blender until thoroughly blended. Pour it back into the pan, add the lemon juice and cook slowly again for a while until it is nice and hot. Serve in soup bowls and sprinkle the minced parsley on top.

 his soup can be served hot during the cold months, or it can be refrigerated and served cold during the summer months.

God does not die on the day when we cease to believe in a personal deity, but we die on the day when our lives cease to be illuminated by the steady radiance renewed daily, of a wonder, the source of which is beyond all reason.

DAG HAMMARSKJÖLD
MARKINGS

SEVILLE GAZPACHO
GAZPACHO SÉVILLAN

6 servings

> **3 large tomatoes**
> **2 cucumbers**
> **1 large green pepper**
> **2 red onions**
> **8 cups water**
> **4 garlic cloves, minced**
> **1/3 cup fresh parsley, finely chopped**
> **2 slices stale bread, crumbled**
> **1/2 cup olive oil**
> **3 Tbsps celery leaves, well chopped**
> **salt and freshly ground pepper to taste**
> **1/2 cup dry sherry**
> **1 Tbsp wine vinegar**

1. Place the tomatoes in water in a large casserole and bring the water to boil for a few minutes. Remove the tomatoes. Peel and seed them. Dice and place on a separate plate.

2. Peel and dice the cucumbers. Sprinkle some salt on them and set aside. Dice the green pepper and set aside. Peel and dice the onion and set aside.

3. Bring the water to boil in a large saucepan, add half of the diced tomatoes and onion, the garlic, parsley, stale bread, olive oil, celery leaves, salt, and pepper; boil over medium heat for about 20 to 25 minutes. Let cool. Add the dry sherry and vinegar and pass the soup through the blender until thoroughly blended. Refrigerate for at least 4 hours.

4. When the time comes to serve the soup, place the rest of the diced tomatoes, pepper, cucumbers, and onion on separate dishes. Pass them around the table so each person can add more of these vegetables to their gazpacho according to their taste.

This is a lovely soup to serve during the summer months. The secret of it is to serve it as cold as possible. It is an ideal dish to serve when one has a table full of guests.

CREAMY CHERVIL SOUP
POTAGE AU CERFEUIL

4 servings

3 leeks (white part only)
1/4 cup celery, chopped
2 Tbsps butter or margarine
4 potatoes, peeled and diced
1 qt water
1 1/2 cups fresh chervil, chopped
1 cup whole milk
salt and freshly ground pepper to taste

1. Slice the leeks and the celery in thin pieces. Melt the butter in a soup pot. Add the leeks, celery, and potatoes, and sauté them for 2 or 3 minutes. Add the water and cook the soup over medium-low heat 20 to 25 minutes until the soup is done.

2. When the soup is done, add the chervil and the remaining ingredients. Purée the soup with a masher (or pass it through a blender). Bring the soup to another boil while stirring constantly and serve immediately. It can also be refrigerated for a few hours and served cold during the summer months.

Economy is the art of making the most of life.
The love of economy is the root of all virtue.

GEORGE BERNARD SHAW

LEBANESE BULGUR WHEAT SALAD

TABBOULÉ

4-6 servings

4 ozs bulgur wheat
2 medium cucumbers, diced
1/2 cup parsley, chopped
1/4 cup mint leaves, chopped
3 shallots, well chopped (or 1 small onion)
4 Tbsps chives, chopped and minced
4 Tbsps olive oil
2 Tbsps lemon juice
salt and pepper to taste

1. Soak the bulgur wheat in cold water for about 1 hour. After the hour, drain thoroughly of every drop of water. Place the bulgur wheat in a salad bowl and refrigerate for another hour.

2. Before serving, add the cucumbers, parsley, mint, shallots, and chives. Pour the olive oil and lemon juice over all. Add salt and pepper, and mix very well. Serve cold.

This dish comes to us from the Middle East and can be served as a delicious appetizer for lunch during the warm days of summer. This salad may be served on Boston lettuce leaves and garnished with olives and tomato slices.

> *One must summer and winter*
> *with the land*
> *and wait its occasions.*
>
> MARY AUSTIN
> *THE LAND OF LITTLE RAIN*

Beets Provençal Style

BETTERAVES À LA PROVENÇALE

6 servings

2 large onions
6 Tbsps olive oil
1 lb fresh beets
2-oz can anchovies
2 tsps Dijon mustard
2 tsps vinegar
white pepper to taste
salt (optional)

1. Peel and chop the onions. Pour 3 tablespoons of olive oil into a frying pan and gently sauté the onions over medium heat for about 4 minutes. Let them cool.

2. Peel the beets and cut them in even thin slices. Place them in a saucepan with water and let them boil for about 3 minutes. Drain and let them cool. Let them cool. (They may be refrigerated for 1 hour.)

3. Purée the onions and the anchovies in a shredder or a blender. Pour this mixture into a deep bowl. Add the remaining olive oil, mustard, vinegar, pepper, and, if necessary, a pinch of salt. Mix thoroughly.

4. Pour this sauce over the beets and mix them well. Serve cold.

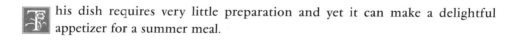 his dish requires very little preparation and yet it can make a delightful appetizer for a summer meal.

SPINACH MADRID STYLE
EPINARDS À LA MADRILÈNE

6 servings

3 lbs fresh spinach
6 hard-boiled eggs
vinaigrette (page 214)

1. Prepare the vinaigrette.

2. Cook the spinach in enough water to cover for about 10 to 12 minutes. Drain well and allow to cool. Cut the spinach leaves several times and place them in a large salad bowl. Add the vinaigrette and toss.

3. Peel and slice the eggs in four from top to bottom, spread the spinach evenly on a flat serving dish and decorate the top with the hard-boiled eggs. Serve chilled.

This dish, together with a cream soup, cheese, and fresh fruit, can make a delightful lunch. Otherwise, it can be served at dinner, as an appetizer or as a salad after the main dish.

Light looked down and beheld Darkness.
"Thither will I go," said Light.
Peace looked down and beheld War.
"Thither will I go," said Peace.
Love looked down and beheld Hatred.
"Thither will I go," said Love.

So came Light and shone.
So came Peace and gave rest.
So came Love and brought life.
LAURENCE HOUSMAN (1865-1959)

Avocado Mousse

MOUSSE D'AVOCATS

6 servings

1 1/2 Tbsps unflavored gelatin
1/3 cup water
2 cups well-mashed avocado pulp (about 4 medium-sized fruits)
1/4 cup lemon juice
pinch garlic salt
1 Tbsp mustard
1 cup heavy cream, beaten stiff
salt to taste
lettuce and tomatoes, for garnish

1. In a bowl mix the gelatin with 3 tablespoons of water. Let it stand for 15 minutes. Then boil the rest of the water and stir to dissolve the gelatin.

2. Place the avocado in a deep bowl and mash and blend it with the lemon juice, garlic salt, mustard, and salt. Mix it with the dissolved gelatin, stirring continuously, and then fold it slowly into the stiffly beaten cream.

3. Grease a flat one-quart ovenproof dish with vegetable oil and gently pour the mixture into it. Cover with aluminum foil and chill the dish overnight or at least 8 hours. When it is ready, cut the mousse into 6 slices and place each on top of a wide leaf of lettuce with sliced tomatoes around as a garnish. Serve cold.

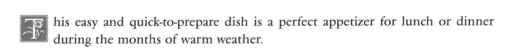 his easy and quick-to-prepare dish is a perfect appetizer for lunch or dinner during the months of warm weather.

STEWED PEPPERS WITH CAPERS
POIVRONS AUX CÂPRES

4-6 servings

6 large tomatoes
6 Tbsps olive oil
3 large green peppers, seeded and sliced in quarters
3 large red peppers, seeded and sliced in quarters
1 large onion, diced
2 garlic cloves, minced
1/2 cup black olives, coarsely chopped
1/2 cup parsley, chopped
1/3 cup basil (preferably fresh), chopped
3 Tbsps capers
dash of tabasco sauce
salt and pepper to taste

1. Wash and boil the tomatoes whole. Peel and slice them.

2. Heat the olive oil in a good-sized heavy skillet. Add the peppers, onion, and garlic. Cook for about 3 to 4 minutes, stirring continually so nothing burns. Add the tomatoes and the rest of the ingredients and continue cooking for 6 to 8 minutes, stirring constantly. Cover the skillet and simmer over low heat for 12 to 15 minutes. Serve warm or at room temperature.

This is a hearty and delicious appetizer to be served at the beginning of any meal, accompanied by plenty of French bread. It may also be served during the main course accompanying a fish, egg, or meat dish.

No man can safely speak,
unless he who would gladly remain silent.
THOMAS À KEMPIS

Saint Fiacre Stuffed Onions

OIGNIONS FARCIS SAINT FIACRE

8 servings

8 medium-sized onions, peeled
4 ozs breadcrumbs
4 ozs grated Romano cheese
1 tomato, peeled and finely chopped
1 tsp dried thyme
1 egg, beaten
5 Tbsps milk
salt and pepper to taste

1. Boil the onions for about 3 to 4 minutes. Drain them and allow to cool. When cool, slice them in perfect halves. With a small thin knife remove the inside of the onions, being careful to keep onion shells or cavities intact.

2. In a deep bowl, mix well the breadcrumbs, cheese, chopped tomato, and thyme. In a separate bowl, mix well the beaten egg, milk, salt, and pepper. Add this mixture to the breadcrumbs and cheese mixture; blend well all ingredients.

3. Fill the onion shells with the mixture.

4. Butter thoroughly an elongated overproof dish. Carefully place the stuffed onions in it. Place the dish in a 300° F oven for 30 minutes. Serve the stuffed onions hot, either as an appetizer or as an accompaniment to the main course (2 halves per person).

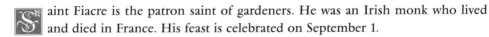 aint Fiacre is the patron saint of gardeners. He was an Irish monk who lived and died in France. His feast is celebrated on September 1.

MAIN DISHES

Spinach Cheese Croquettes
Croquettes des Epinards au Fromage

4 servings

1 onion, diced
2 eggs
1 cup spinach, chopped and cooked
1 cup breadcrumbs
1 Tbsp vegetable oil
1 tsp lemon juice
1 cup Parmesan cheese, grated
salt and pepper to taste
vegetable oil for deep frying
flour

1. Lightly sauté the diced onion. Beat one egg in a deep bowl. Add the onion, spinach (drained of all water), and breadcrumbs. Mix and blend these very well. Then add the cheese, lemon juice, 1 tablespoon oil, salt, and pepper; mix thoroughly. Place this mixture in the refrigerator for at least 1 hour.

2. Beat another egg. Remove the spinach mixture from the refrigerator and form into small balls about 2 1/2 inches wide. Dip the rolls into the beaten egg, and then roll them in flour. Fry them in hot oil until they turn golden brown. Drain them on a paper towel and serve them hot. It should yield about 8 to 10 croquettes.

Pray without ceasing
God hears what you say
From the moment you rise
To the close of each day.
Don't think for a moment
That he turns a deaf ear.
Trust and have faith
And you'll never know fear.

HELEN PARKER

Purée of Eggplant
PAPETON

4-6 servings

3 lbs eggplant
6 Tbsps olive oil, more if needed
1 tsp thyme, minced
1 tsp rosemary, minced
4 eggs
1 cup milk
salt and pepper to taste

1. Peel the eggplants and cut them into slices. Place them in a bowl with salty water for 30 minutes. Remove and dry thoroughly.

2. Pour olive oil into a frying pan and place the eggplant into it. Sprinkle the thyme and rosemary over the eggplant. Lower the heat to medium low. Cover the pan and allow the eggplant to cook for about 15 minutes.

3. Beat the eggs and add the milk. Mix well. Add salt and pepper and mix some more.

4. Use a masher to crush the eggplants and add them to the egg mixture. Mix thoroughly. Generously grease an earthenware mold and pour the eggplant mixture into it. Cook in the oven at 350° F for 45 minutes. When done, unmold onto a flat round dish and serve. One can also serve freshly made tomato sauce on the side. It adds color and taste to the eggplant.

 apeton is a specialty of Avignon in France where it was originally cooked in a mold shaped like the papal crown.

GRATIN OF VEGETABLES
GRATIN DE LÉGUMES

4 servings

4 medium-sized turnips
4 medium-sized carrots
1 small 8- to 12-oz can sweet corn
4 Tbsps milk
8 Tbsps butter
3 large tomatoes
1 cup breadcrumbs
salt and pepper to taste

1. Peel and slice the turnips and carrots. Place them in a casserole of boiling water, and let them cook for about 20 to 25 minutes. Add salt at the end.

2. Rinse the canned sweet corn and place it in a large bowl. Add the milk and 4 tablespoons of butter.

3. Wash the tomatoes and slice them evenly.

4. When the turnips and carrots are well cooked, rinse and drain them completely. Then mash them with a fork into a solid purée. Pour the purée into the bowl containing the sweet corn. Add some fresh pepper and mix everything very well.

5. Butter a long flat dish for the gratin and pour the vegetable mixture into it. Cover evenly with the sliced tomatoes. Sprinkle with the breadcrumbs. Cut into tiny pieces the remaining 4 tablespoons of butter and distribute evenly on top of the dish.

6. Place the dish in a preheated oven of about 350° F for about 15 minutes. Then take it out and place the dish under the broiler until the topping looks golden brown (about 5 minutes). Allow it to cool a bit and serve.

The monk is compassionate in proportion as he is less practical and less successful, because the job of being a success in a competitive society leaves one no time for compassion. The monk has all the more of a part to play in our world, because he has no proper place in it.

THOMAS MERTON

BASQUE STEWED VEGETABLES WITH EGGS
PIPERADE SIMPLE

4 servings

2 zucchini, sliced
4 tomatoes, peeled
2 peppers, diced
2 medium-sized onions, diced
6 Tbsps olive oil
2 garlic cloves, minced
6 eggs
1/4 cup whole milk
salt and pepper to taste
minced parsley (optional)

1. Sauté the zucchini, tomatoes, peppers, and onions in the olive oil in a good-sized skillet over medium heat. Add the well-minced garlic. Cook until the vegetables are tender.

2. In a large bowl, beat the eggs, milk, salt, and pepper.

3. Pour the egg mixture over the vegetables and cook over slow heat, stirring continuously until all the liquid has disappeared. The dish is ready when the creamy moist mixture becomes firm and thick. Be careful not to burn or overcook it. Sprinkle some parsley over each portion and serve it hot.

When people come together who have not previously met, they are a bit reserved; but when food is introduced there is an immediate change in the atmosphere. The power of the festive table begins to operate, bringing a feeling of gentleness and warmth. What I am trying to convey is that we have to begin somewhere to relate to the environment. How better than with food?

ALAN HOOKER
VEGETARIAN GOURMET COOKERY

CASSEROLE OF CORN AND EGGS
GRATIN DE MAIS

4-6 servings

> **5 ears fresh corn or 1 lb frozen corn**
> **1 large onion**
> **4 tomatoes**
> **2 green bell peppers**
> **4 to 6 Tbsps vegetable oil**
> **4 eggs**
> **1/2 cup milk**
> **salt and pepper to taste**
> **1/2 lb mozzarella cheese, grated**

1. In a good-sized saucepan boil the ears of corn for about 5 to 6 minutes, until they are tender. Rinse them in cold water and with a sharp knife remove kernels from cob carefully.

2. Peel and thinly slice the onion, tomatoes, and peppers. Sauté them in vegetable oil in a large frying pan until they turn into sauce.

3. In a large bowl beat the eggs, adding the milk, salt, and pepper; mix very well.

4. Add one half of the mozzarella cheese, or any other of your favorite cheeses.

5. Pour the corn and the tomato sauce into the bowl with the egg mixture. Add the remaining cheese and mix the entire thing very well. Pour this mixture into a large flat well-buttered dish, and bake in the oven at 350° F for about 30 minutes. It is ready when the mixture becomes consistently solid. Serve it hot.

his recipe is one of those that provides a completely nutritious meal in itself and can be served as the main dish. The secret to the success of this dish is the use of the fresh sweet corn, readily available during the summer months.

THREE-COLORED VEGETABLE STEW
RAGOUT DE LÉGUMES A TROIS COULEURS

4 servings

    4 potatoes, peeled
    3 carrots, peeled
    2 zucchini
    1 large onion
    3 Tbsps olive oil
    1 Tbsp flour
    1/2 cup fresh parsley, finely minced
    2 1/2 cups boiling water
    salt and pepper to taste

1. Slice the potatoes, carrots, zucchini, and onion.

2. In a medium-sized saucepan, fry the sliced onion in olive oil until it becomes light brown. Add the flour and the boiling water. Stir to form a thin sauce.

3. Add the finely minced parsley and the potatoes, carrots, zucchini, salt, and pepper.

4. Cover the saucepan and cook slowly over low heat for 30 minutes, stirring the contents occasionally. Serve it hot. It is a delicious and filling dish.

ther vegetables may be substituted in this dish. For instance, yellow summer squash or green string beans can be used instead of zucchini.

Animals feed themselves; men eat;
but only wise men know the art of eating.
ANTHELME BRILLAT-SAVARIN

Swiss Chard Basque Style
BLETTES LA BASQUAISE

6 servings

> **6 cups Swiss chard stalks, cut 3 inches long**
> **6 garlic cloves, finely minced**
> **1/3 cup olive oil**
> **1/4 cup wine vinegar**
> **salt and pepper to taste**

1. Cook the Swiss chard stalks in a double boiler for about 15 minutes. Prick with a fork to check for tenderness, although they should remain rather firm. Do not overcook them.

2. When the Swiss chard is ready, gently rub the minced garlic into a large saucepan or skillet, pressing the garlic from time to time into the pan. Pour the olive oil into the pan and raise the heat to medium-high for about 1 or 2 minutes. Add the Swiss chard, vinegar (or wine), salt and pepper. Carefully toss the vegetables for another minute or two. Cover the pan until ready to serve. Serve hot.

Swiss chard is a much-used vegetable in France where there are endless ways of preparing it, and where many people prefer it to spinach. When one travels around France, one sees chard growing in rows in small-home gardens, in large-kitchen gardens in monasteries, and in fields of cultivation. Unfortunately this vegetable has not caught as much the imagination of American producers. It is rare when one can find it in the local supermarket. However, since it grows easily, all home gardeners should take advantage and cultivate it for their summer and fall consumption and then freeze some for the winter months.

And so I saw full surely that before ever God made us, God loved us. And this love was never quenched nor ever shall be. And in this love God has done all works, and made all things profitable to us, and in this love our life is everlasting. In our making we had beginning, but the love in which God made us was in God from without beginning.

JULIAN OF NORWICH

EGGPLANT SICILIAN STYLE
AUBERGINES SICILIENNES

6 servings

6 medium-sized eggplants
1 large onion, sliced
6 tomatoes, peeled and crushed
3 garlic cloves, minced
olive oil
salt
grated Romano cheese
basil and oregano (optional)

1. Wash the eggplants and cut them in half lengthwise. Use a fork to make some incisions in the cut surface.

2. Pour some oil into a large saucepan. Place the eggplants upside down in the oil and cook for about five minutes, watching that they do not burn. Let them cool. With a sharp knife and a pointed spoon, scoop the pulp out onto a separate plate, keeping the shell intact.

3. Pour some oil into a large frying pan. Add the onion, garlic, and tomatoes and sauté them over medium heat for 6 to 7 minutes. Add the eggplant pulp and salt, and sauté for about 2 or 3 minutes more.

4. Fill the eggplant shell halves with this sauce. Place them in a well-buttered flat ovenproof dish. Sprinkle the top with grated cheese and bake at 350° F for about 10 to 15 minutes until they are done. Serve hot.

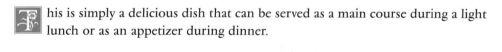his is simply a delicious dish that can be served as a main course during a light lunch or as an appetizer during dinner.

Saint Daniel's Fettuccine
Fettuccine San Daniele

4 servings

> **2 qts water**
> **10 ozs fettucine**
> **1/2 cup olive oil**
> **8 cloves garlic, finely minced**
> **4 tsps basil, chopped and minced**
> **8 ozs black pitted olives, finely chopped**
> **salt and pepper to taste**
> **grated Romano cheese**
> **1/2 cup heavy cream**

1. Bring the water to a boil and cook the fettucine for about 5 to 8 minutes, being watchful that they are not overcooked and that they remain *al dente*.

2. Meanwhile, pour the olive oil into a blender. Add the garlic, chopped basil, salt, and pepper; mix everything very well. Pour the contents of the mixer into a skillet. Add the black olives and the heavy cream. Cook briefly over medium heat, stirring continually

3. Drain the fettucine and place in a large serving bowl. Pour the sauce on top and toss. Sprinkle with the grated cheese on the top and serve it very hot.

This recipe can be used with other sorts of pasta, like a thin spaghetti, if, for instance, fettuccine is not available. Because of the better quality it is always best to use Italian imported fettuccine, unless, of course, one makes one's own. A robust Italian red wine accompanies this dish very well.

> *If an Arab in the desert were suddenly to discover a spring in his tent, and so would always be able to have water in abundance, how fortunate he would consider himself—so too, when a man, who as a physical being is always turned toward the outside, thinking that his happiness lies outside him, finally turns inward and discovers that the source is within him; not to mention his discovery that the source is his relation to God.*
>
> Søren Kierkegaard

CARROTS WITH RAISINS
CAROTTES AUX RAISINS

6 servings

> **8 large carrots**
> **20 small white onions**
> **4 Tbsps butter**
> **3 cups fruity white wine**
> **1 bay leaf**
> **pinch dried thyme**
> **pinch cayenne pepper**
> **salt and pepper to taste**
> **3/4 cup mixed raisins (dark and light)**

1. Wash and peel the carrots. Slice them three inches long. (You can also use whole baby carrots if they are available.) Peel the small onions carefully so they remain intact.

2. Melt the butter in a good-sized saucepan and immediately add the onions and carrots. Shake the saucepan thoroughly so the vegetables are evenly coated with the butter. Add the salt, pepper, thyme, cayenne, and bay leaf. Add the raisins, scattering them over the vegetables, then pour the wine over all. Bring to a boil, cover the pan, and then let it simmer for one hour over low heat. Stir gently two or three times to see that the carrots are evenly cooked. Serve hot.

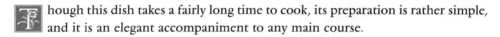

Though this dish takes a fairly long time to cook, its preparation is rather simple, and it is an elegant accompaniment to any main course.

Let us strive to make the present moment beautiful.

SAINT FRANCIS DE SALES

Vegetables Mediterranean Style

LÉGUMES LA MÉDITERRANÉENNE

6 servings

> 2 onions
> 2 red peppers
> 1/2 cup olive oil
> 1 cup dry sherry
> 1/2 cup water
> 2 zucchini
> 12 asparagus, cut in 2-inch lengths
> 12 pitted olives
> 24 mushrooms, sliced
> pinch of freshly ground black pepper
> salt to taste
> 1/3 cup minced fresh parsley

1. Slice the onions and peppers. Pour the oil into a saucepan and gently sauté the onions and peppers for about 3 minutes. Add the sherry and water. Stir.

2. In the meantime, quarter the zucchini lengthwise and then slice them 2 inches long. Add the zucchini, asparagus, olives, and mushrooms to the onion and pepper sauce. Add salt and pepper and stir. Then cover the pan and cook slowly over low heat until most of the liquid is absorbed. Stir from time to time so it doesn't burn at the bottom.

3. When the vegetables are almost ready, add the parsley, stir well and continue cooking for another 3 to 4 minutes. Serve hot during the cold months or refrigerate for a few hours and serve cold as an appetizer.

He has spent his life best who has enjoyed it most. God will take care that we do not enjoy it any more than is good for us.

SAMUEL BUTLER

Stuffed Tomatoes Provençal Style
Tomatoes a la Provençale

8 servings

8 good-sized firm tomatoes
8 Tbsps olive oil
1 onion, finely chopped
6 garlic cloves, finely minced
4 Tbsps fresh parsley, finely chopped
4 Tbsps fresh basil, finely chopped
2 tsps thyme
2 tsps rosemary
2 eggs
1/3 cup whole milk
1 cup breadcrumbs
salt and pepper to taste
grated Parmesan cheese

1. Wash and rinse the tomatoes. Cut them at the top, just a little below the stem and carefully scoop out the pulp with a small spoon.

2. Heat the oil in a large skillet, then add the tomato pulp, onion, garlic, and the finely chopped and minced herbs. Sauté for a few minutes until all ingredients are well blended.

3. In a deep bowl beat the egg with the milk, add the contents of the skillet, the breadcrumbs, salt, and pepper. Mix very well and fill the empty tomatoes with this mixture. Sprinkle the top of the tomatoes with grated cheese. Grease a flat baking dish and delicately place the tomatoes on it. Bake them at 350° F for 30 minutes.

This is a colorful and appetizing dish well known to all those who have traveled throughout Provence. The magic combination of tomatoes and herbs, which grow all over the countryside of Provence, is typically identified in this dish. There are endless variations on this basic recipe, but no matter what recipe one may choose, the fragrant herbs from Provence must be there. It can be served as an attractive appetizer or as a delicious accompaniment to any fish, meat, or egg dish.

EGGPLANT PÂTÉ
PÂTÉ D'AUBERGINES

6 servings

>   2 medium-sized eggplants
>   1 sweet red pepper
>   2 onions
>   1/4 cup olive oil
>   4 garlic cloves, minced
>   1 bay leaf
>   mixed herbs (thyme, basil, rosemary)
>   salt and pepper to taste
>   1/2 cup heavy cream
>   capers (optional)

1. Dice the eggplant, pepper, and onion.

2. Pour the olive oil in a large skillet. Add the eggplant, pepper, onion, garlic, bay leaf, mixed herbs, salt, and pepper; sauté them slowly over medium heat. Turn them often. Don't let the vegetables stick to the bottom of the pan. Add a bit of water, if needed. Cover the pan and let it simmer for about 15 minutes. Remove bay leaf.

3. Mash the vegetables or purée them in a blender. Pour the mixture into a deep bowl, add the cream, and blend everything well by hand. Place the mixture in a flat buttered baking dish. Bake at 300° F for about 25 to 30 minutes. This dish may be served hot or cold.

his pâté can be served in a variety of ways. It can be used, for example, as a spread over thin slices of toasted French bread. It can also be served as a simple hors d'oeuvre, or one can carefully hollow out some tomatoes and stuff them with this mixture and bake them also at 300° F for 30 minutes. The result is something like Stuffed Tomatoes Provençal Style (see previous recipe).

The enclosure of a monastery profits only those who love it and who desire and seek not the perishable goods of this world but those that are eternal.

SAINT MARGARET OF HUNGARY

Green String Beans Saint Jacques

HARICOTS-VERTS SAINT-JACQUES

4-6 servings

1 lb green string beans
2 qts water
4 red sweet peppers or pimentos
6 Tbsps olive oil
4 garlic cloves, minced
salt and pepper to taste

1. Wash and clean the fresh string beans. Bring 2 quarts water to boil in a large saucepan, add the beans, cover the pan, and continue boiling over medium heat until the beans are tender. Don't overdo it, for the beans must remain firm. Fresh beans from the garden will cook more quickly than beans from the market. When the beans are tender enough, drain them, and set them aside.

2. While the beans are boiling, clean the red peppers and cut them in half. Remove the seeds. Butter a flat baking dish, place the peppers on it, outside up and press them flat to the dish. Place the dish under the broiler and thus cook the peppers until they are entirely roasted. Peel and slice them.

3. Pour olive oil into a large skillet, add the minced garlic and the roasted peppers and sauté them gently for about 1 to 2 minutes. Stir continually. Then add the beans and continue to stir over medium-low heat for another 2 minutes. Turn off the heat and cover the pan until it is time to serve. Add salt and pepper. Serve hot.

A rather unusual and yet delicious way of preparing fresh string beans. This dish can be served either as an appetizer or it can nicely accompany the main course of either fish, meat, or eggs.

> *My soul can find no staircase to Heaven*
> *unless it be through Earth's loveliness.*
> MICHELANGELO

Couscous With Mediterranean Sauce
Couscous à la méditerranéenne

4 servings

For the sauce:
   1/2 cup olive oil
   1 large onion, chopped
   4 fresh tomatoes, peeled and chopped (or 1 lb canned tomatoes)
   1 bell pepper, chopped
   3 garlic cloves, minced
   1 medium-sized zucchini, cut in 3-inch lengths
   7 ozs artichoke hearts (canned or frozen)
   7 ozs pitted black olives
   herbs, minced (basil and thyme)
   salt and pepper to taste

For the couscous:
   1 1/2 cups water
   2 vegetable bouillon cubes
   4 Tbsps olive oil
   1 cup couscous
   salt to taste

1. Pour the olive oil into a deep pan and sauté the onion, tomatoes, and pepper lightly until they achieve the consistency of a sauce. Add the garlic, zucchini, artichoke hearts, black olives, minced herbs, salt, and pepper. Cover the pan and continue cooking the sauce over low heat for about 7 to 8 minutes, stirring from time to time. Then simmer the sauce gently for another 7 minutes.

2. While the sauce is simmering, prepare the couscous. Pour the water into a large saucepan, add the bouillon cubes and bring the water to a boil. Add the olive oil, couscous, and salt. Stir well and cover. Cook over a very low flame for about 3 minutes. Remove from the heat and let it stand another 5 minutes. Pour the sauce over the couscous and serve hot.

ouscous is a Mediterranean dish of Arab origin that has become quite popular these days throughout France and continental Europe. It is a sort of fine-grained pasta made of semolina and water. It comes in packages mostly imported from France, but it is beginning to be produced in the United States along with some other foods from the Near East, such as falafel. Couscous is extremely simple to prepare and it is a delightful change from the usual diet of potato, rice, or macaroni dishes. Since the sauce takes longer to prepare, it should be made first, and then prepare the couscous while the sauce is simmering, just before serving.

To live selflessly is to live in joy,
realizing by experience that life itself
is love and a gift. To be a lover and a giver
is to be a channel through which the
Supreme Giver manifests His Love in the world.
THOMAS MERTON

Saint Germaine Risotto
RISSOTTO SAINTE GERMAINE

4 servings

- **4 Tbsps olive oil**
- **1 onion, finely chopped**
- **2 garlic cloves, finely chopped and minced**
- **1 medium-sized zucchini, cut into half-inch cubes**
- **2 medium-sized red peppers, seeded and cut into small cubes**
- **1 cup arborio rice**
- **1 tsp dried thyme**
- **1 bay leaf**
- **1/2 tsp paprika**
- **2 cups boiling water**
- **salt and freshly ground pepper to taste**

1. Heat the oil in a good-sized saucepan. Add the onion, garlic, zucchini, and peppers. Stir for about 2 minutes over low-medium heat.

2. Add the rice. Stir and blend well. After a minute or so, add the thyme, bay leaf, and paprika; stir some more. Gradually add the boiling water, salt, and pepper; continue stirring until all ingredients are evenly mixed.

3. Cover the saucepan tightly and let the risotto simmer gently, stirring from time to time until all the liquid part is absorbed. Uncover, remove the bay leaf, and stir lightly. Serve the risotto hot.

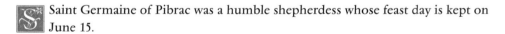 Saint Germaine of Pibrac was a humble shepherdess whose feast day is kept on June 15.

SALADS

POTATO SALAD
SALADE PARMENTIER

4 servings

8 to 10 medium-sized potatoes
1/2 cup dry white wine
1 bunch of chervil
3 sprigs of tarragon
8 to 10 Tbsps olive oil
salt and pepper to taste

1. Wash the potatoes and let them cook in salted boiling water for exactly 20 minutes. Peel and cut them in even chunks. Place the potatoes in a deep salad bowl and pour the white wine over them. Mix the potatoes delicately and allow them to cool.

2. In the meantime, cut and finely mince the chervil and tarragon. Place the herbs in a cup, add olive oil, a pinch of salt, and fresh pepper. Add to the potato mixture; mix delicately. Place the salad bowl in the refrigerator for one hour before serving. Serve cold.

This quick and simple-to-prepare potato salad is a welcome variation from the everyday common potato salad. It can be served as an appetizer, or it can accompany the main dish.

> *A certain brother went to Abbot Moses in Skete, and asked him for a good word. And the elder said to him: Go, sit in your cell, and your cell will teach you everything.*
>
> THE WISDOM OF THE DESERT

MACARONI SALAD ITALIAN STYLE
SALADE DE MACARONI À L'ITALIENNE

6-8 servings

    1 cup homemade mayonnaise (see page 215)
    1 lb macaroni
    3 hard-boiled eggs, peeled and chopped
    1 medium-sized onion, chopped and minced
    7-oz jar pimentos, sliced
    14-oz jar pitted black or green olives, sliced
    salt and pepper to taste

1. Prepare the mayonnaise.

2. Drop the macaroni into boiling water and let them cook gently, stirring from time to time. Don't let them overcook. Drain and rinse them in cold water. Drain them again and let them cool.

3. Place the macaroni in a deep glass or earthenware salad bowl. Add the hard-boiled eggs, onion, pimentos, olives, and mayonnaise (or the same amount of the commercial type). Add salt and pepper. Mix well and chill for at least 2 hours before serving. Serve very cold.

We possess God, not in the sense that we become exactly as He, but in that we approach Him as closely as possible in a miraculous, spiritual manner, and that our innermost being is illuminated and seized by His truth and His Holiness.

SAINT AUGUSTINE

SURPRISE SALAD
SALADE SURPRISE

4-6 servings

1 sweet red pepper
1 heart of celery
1 medium-sized onion
8-oz jar artichoke hearts
2 cups fresh corn, (or frozen or canned)
2 hard-boiled eggs, peeled and sliced
mayonnaise or vinaigrette (see pages 214–215)

1. Cut the red pepper in big slices and place under the broiler for a few minutes until they become tender. Peel them and slice into small pieces.

2. Slice the celery, onion, and artichoke hearts into small pieces; add the drained corn with the thinly sliced red pepper in a deep bowl. Mix well. Add the mayonnaise or the vinaigrette and mix thoroughly. Place the sliced hard-boiled eggs on top and put it in the refrigerator for 2 hours. Serve cold.

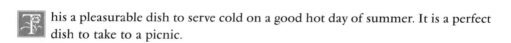 his a pleasurable dish to serve cold on a good hot day of summer. It is a perfect dish to take to a picnic.

LENTIL SALAD
SALADE DE LENTILLES

6-8 servings

1 lb lentils, black or green
1 bunch fresh radishes
1 large red onion or 4 shallots
3 stalks fresh celery
8 to 10 capers
vinaigrette with mustard (see page 214)

1. Place the lentils in a large saucepan with 2 quarts boiling water. Let them boil for 15 minutes. It is important, however, that the lentils not be over-cooked or mushy and that they remain firm. Drain them in cold water.

2. Dice the radishes, onion, and celery in small thin pieces. Place them and the lentils in a deep bowl. Mix them thoroughly. Place the bowl in the refrigerator until just before serving.

3. Prepare the vinaigrette; add the capers. Blend thoroughly and pour over the salad before serving. Toss and serve immediately.

The Christian is cheerful, easy, kind, gentle, courteous, candid, unassuming; without pretense, affectation, ambition, or singularity, because the Christian has neither hope nor fear about this world. Serious, sober, discreet, grave, moderate, mild, with so little that is unusual or striking in his or her bearing, the Christian may easily be taken for an ordinary person.

JOHN HENRY NEWMAN

SALAD OF THE ISLANDS
SALADE DES ILES

4 servings

> **4 tomatoes**
> **2 avocados**
> **1 jar or can of small onions (around 2 ozs)**
> **vinaigrette (see page 214)**

1. Cut the tomatoes in round slices and place them on a flat round plate, covering the entire plate.

2. Peel the avocados. Cut one in 8 long slices and dice the other in small cubes. Drain the onions of all the water and cut the larger ones in half.

3. Place the 8 avocado slices on top of the tomatoes, at equal distance from one another. Place the avocado dices in between the long slices, and place the onions in the very center of the plate. It should look attractively decorated.

4. Pour the vinaigrette over the entire salad just before serving.

This attractive dish can be served as an appetizer before the main course, especially in midsummer when the tomatoes are in season.

RICE SALAD WITH TUNA FISH
SALADE DE RIZ AU THON

4 servings

1 cup long-grain rice
2 cups water
1 medium-sized onion
8-oz can tuna fish, drained
8 Tbsps mayonnaise (see page 215)
salt and pepper to taste
a few drops of lemon juice (optional)

1. Boil the rice in 2 cups of water until it is well done and all water is evaporated.

2. Slice the onion and mince it finely; drain the juice and then mince the tuna finely.

3. Place the rice, onion, and tuna fish in a large bowl. Add the mayonnaise, a pinch of salt and pepper, and a few drops of lemon juice. Mix everything very well and place the bowl in the refrigerator for two hours or more. Serve cold.

This dish is wonderful on a hot summer day or for a lovely picnic in the country. It can also be used as an appetizer before dinner served with sliced tomatoes and cucumbers on the side. Those who are not vegetarians and prefer something else to tuna fish could substitute the same amount of deviled ham.

The Kingdom of Heaven, O people, requires no other price than yourselves,
the value of it is yourselves. Give yourselves for it and you shall have it.
SAINT AUGUSTINE

Russian Salad
SALADE À LA RUSSE

6 servings

For the salad:
   1 lb potatoes
   4 large tomatoes, cored and quartered
   1 red onion, sliced and separated into rings
   1/2 cup pitted black olives, halved
   4 cornichons (small pickles), thinly sliced (optional)
   3 hard-boiled eggs, peeled and chopped
   12 capers (or more according to taste)

For the dressing:
   1 cup mayonnaise (for homemade, see page 215)
   2 Tbsps olive oil
   1 Tbsp tarragon vinegar
   salt and fresh pepper to taste

1. Wash and peel the potatoes. Cut them in medium-sized cubes. Boil for about 8 to 10 minutes. They should be fully cooked yet remain firm. Rinse them in cold water and then drain them.

2. Peel and chop the eggs. Place the potatoes and eggs in a large salad bowl. Add the olives, cornichons, onions, capers, and all the dressing ingredients, except the mayonnaise. Mix carefully but thoroughly. Add the mayonnaise and again mix thoroughly with care. Refrigerate for a few hours and serve the salad cold.

A bowl of fresh, tender leaves from any of half a hundred kinds of garden lettuces, unadorned except for the simplest possible mixture of oil, vinegar and seasonings, is a joy to the palate.

M. F. K. Fisher
The Cooking of Provincial France

DESSERTS

MELON WITH STRAWBERRIES
CANTALOUPS AUX FRAISES

6 servings

> **3 small sweet melons**
> **1 lb fresh strawberries**
> **1/3 cup Port wine**
> **sugar to taste**

1. Choose 3 melons in season, cut them in half, and clean the insides well.

2. Wash the strawberries and if they are too big, cut them in two or three parts. Place them in a good-sized bowl. Add the Port wine and sugar and mix gently. Put the bowl and the melons in the refrigerator until it is time to serve.

3. At dessert time, fill each melon half with the strawberries. Serve chilled.

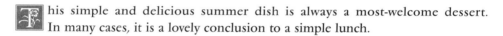 his simple and delicious summer dish is always a most-welcome dessert. In many cases, it is a lovely conclusion to a simple lunch.

PEACH MOUSSE
MOUSSE DE PÊCHE

6 servings

> **1 lb fresh peaches, peeled and pitted, or a 1-lb can of peaches, drained**
> **3 Tbsps peach brandy**
> **1/2 pint heavy cream**
> **1/3 cup confectioners' sugar**

1. Pass the peaches through a blender until smooth. They should amount to about 4 full cups.

2. Pour the cream in a deep bowl and add the sugar and brandy. Whip until the cream has a thick consistency. Add the peaches and blend the mixture thoroughly.

3. Pour the mixture into 6 dessert glasses and place them in the refrigerator for several hours. The mousse should be served cold.

Oranges for Saint Benedict's Day

ORANGES DE LA SAINT BENOÎT

6 servings

6 navel oranges
1 cup diced candied fruit (mixed)
1/2 cup Kirsch
1/2 cup sugar

Cut the oranges evenly in half and, using a spoon, carefully remove the pulp from the inside, watching to see that the shells remain intact. Remove the seeds and cut the pulp in small tiny pieces. Place them in a deep bowl. Add the diced candied (mixed) fruit, the kirsch, and sugar. Mix everything well and fill the orange shells with this mixture. Bake in a preheated oven at 350° F for about 25 to 30 minutes. Serve warm.

Saint Benedict was born in Nursia, Italy, in 480. He was educated in Rome and later, disgusted with the pleasure-seeking crowd of the city, left for the mountains of Subiaco where he became a hermit. After several years of strict solitary life, a community of monks approached him and asked him to be their abbot. He accepted reluctantly. The monks later refused to accept his strict way of life and tried to poison him. He left them and returned to his beloved solitude of Subiaco. There he again began to receive disciples whom he trained in the ways of monastic life by the use of his Rule and the very example of his life. Soon, Subiaco became a center of monastic discipline, spirituality, and great learning which radiated throughout the whole of Europe. He later settled in Monte Cassino, where be died in about 547.

Saint Benedict is considered the father of Western monasticism because the Rule he wrote shaped European monastic life and European culture for centuries. His Rule, full of wisdom and moderation, a striking balance between prayer, study, and work, has survived the test of the centuries until today. Subiaco and Monte Cassino remain today centers of monastic life, and thousands of monks and nuns around the world still follow in the footsteps of Saint Benedict. Because of the influence of Benedictine monasteries in the formation of European culture, Saint Benedict was rightly given the title of Patron of Europe.

The Transitus of Saint Benedict is celebrated on March 21 and his solemnity on July 11.

CREAM WITH COGNAC
CRÉME AU COGNAC

6 servings

> **1 oz almonds, chopped in small pieces**
> **1 oz rolled oats**
> **1 oz breadcrumbs**
> **1/2 cup heavy cream**
> **4 Tbsps liquid honey**
> **4 Tbsps cognac**
> **5 ozs plain yogurt**

1. Place the almonds, rolled oats, and breadcrumbs in a deep bowl. Mix well. Spread this mixture over a flat ovenproof dish and put under the broiler for a few minutes. Stir frequently and, above all, don't let it burn. Allow it to cool.

2. Pour the heavy cream into a cool deep bowl. Add the honey and cognac and whip with a mixer until the cream thickens. Add the yogurt and the mixture of almonds, oats, and breadcrumbs. Continue mixing and fold it slowly in the stiffly beaten cream.

3. Pour the cream into 6 dessert dishes or cups and refrigerate them for at least 6 hours before serving.

This is a quick and healthy dessert to prepare for friends, and it is particularly appealing during the summer months. If one prefers the cream a bit sweeter, simply add a bit of confectioners' sugar while beating the cream.

Joyful let us drink the sober drunkenness of the spirit.

MONASTIC BREVIARY

MEDLEY OF FOUR FRUITS
MACÉDOINE AUX OUATRE FRUITS

4 servings

7 ozs strawberries (preferably wild strawberries, *fraises des bois*)
7 ozs black cherries
7 ozs currants
7 ozs raspberries
sugar
raspberry (or almond) liqueur

1. Wash and clean the fruit thoroughly. Remove the stems from the fruit. Pit and halve the cherries.

2. Place the fruit in a deep crystal or glass bowl. Add sugar to taste and a few teaspoons of liqueur. Mix well and refrigerate for at least 2 hours before serving. Serve cold.

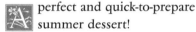 perfect and quick-to-prepare summer dessert!

> *The soul is kissed by God in its innermost regions.*
> *With interior yearning, grace and blessing are bestowed.*
> *It is a yearning to take on God's gentle yoke,*
> *it is a yearning to give one's self to God's way.*
> HILDEGARD OF BINGEN

SAINT SABAS' RASPBERRIES WITH CREAM

FRAMBOISES SAINT-SABAS

6 servings

5 egg yolks
1 cup granulated sugar
1 cup cream sherry
3 cups raspberries
1 cup heavy cream
confectioners' sugar

1. Place the 5 egg yolks into the top of a double boiler. Cook slowly while beating steadily with an eggbeater or a mixer. Add the cup of sugar and beat thoroughly. Pour in the sherry and stir thoroughly with a spoon until the custard becomes thick. Remove from heat. Place the custard in a bowl and allow to cool.

2. Trim, wash, and dry the raspberries. Set aside a few of them to use as a decoration.

3. Just before serving, beat the heavy cream until stiff. Fold the stiff cream into the custard and blend completely. Add the raspberries, turning them carefully with a spoon until they are completely covered by the custard-cream. Place the cream into 6 dessert glasses and refrigerate until it is time to serve. Before serving, dip a few raspberries into the confectioners' sugar and place them on top of each dessert glass. Serve cold.

Saint Sabas was born near Caesarea in Capadocia in 439. He is one of the most remarkable figures of early monasticism and is considered one of the fathers of monastic life. The monastery of "laura" he founded near the Dead Sea, named Mar-Saba after him, was often called the Great Laura because of its reputation for sanctity. Today the monastery is still inhabited by Eastern monks who follow the long tradition of austerity and charity established hundreds of years ago by Saint Sabas. Because of his reputation for holiness, Saint Sabas is called "the pearl from the Orient." His feast is celebrated on December 5.

CHOCOLATE MOUSSE
MOUSSE AU CHOCOLAT

4-6 servings

8 ozs pure chocolate, sliced in small pieces
3 tsps instant coffee
1/3 cup granulated sugar (add more according to taste)
1/2 cup heavy cream
4 egg yolks
1 Tbsp brandy or cognac
4 egg whites

1. Melt the chocolate and the coffee together over low beat using a rubber spatula to stir. One could also melt the chocolate using a double boiler. Let it cool.

2. Beat the sugar and cream in a deep bowl. Set aside.

3. Beat the egg yolks. Add little by little to the chocolate, stirring and beating with a mixer at high speed. Add the brandy and the sugar-cream mixture and continue beating at high speed. Set aside for 5 minutes.

4. Beat the egg whites until they become stiff and firm. Fold the egg whites into the chocolate and blend thoroughly and carefully until no trace of egg whites is seen. Pour the mousse into individual dessert glasses and refrigerate for at least 4 hours before serving.

New every morning is the love
Our wakening and uprising prove;
Through sleep and darkness safely brought,
Restored to life and power and thought.

JOHN KEBLE
CHRISTIAN FEAR

STRAWBERRIES FROM THE JURA
FRAISES À LA JURASIÈNNE

6-8 servings

> **3 lbs strawberries**
> **2 cups ricotta cheese**
> **2 cups heavy cream**
> **1 tsp vanilla extract**
> **1/3 cup confectioners' sugar (optional)**
> **8 ozs strawberry jam**

1. Wash and clean the strawberries. Trim off their stems and cut in half.

2. In a deep bowl mix the cheese, heavy cream, vanilla, and the confectioners' sugar, if desired. Beat thoroughly with an electric mixer.

3. Arrange 6 or 8 dessert bowls. Evenly pour the cream into each. Spread 2 or more tablespoons of strawberry jam on top of the cream. Cover the rest of each dish with fresh strawberries. Refrigerate for 1 hour or more and serve cold.

I cannot be your Spring
I am your Fall.
Spring is full of promises, hope
But it rarely delivers.
A few good days and it jumps into Summer.
Ah! But Fall, Fall lingers.

AUTUMN

For this good food and joy renewed
We praise your name, O Lord.

FRENCH TABLE PRAYER

The quiet and reflective autumn months follow the bustle of summertime and the intense activities associated with it. We sense that autumn is making its appearance when, during the crisp and clear evenings of September, we begin to feel a chill in the air. It is a hint of the arrival of the season that crowns the year with such dramatic changes and colors.

Autumn stands apart by itself—it is not merely a prolongation of summer or a simple prelude to the oncoming winter. Though seemingly it carries something of both within itself. At a certain moment within the season, when the turning of the leaves is at its peak, with bright oranges and yellows, reds and browns, all around us, we see autumn as being distinctly different from all the others, with a glamour and beauty we realize all its own. As we pause to savor the loveliness of the season, we realize that autumn is also a time of transition—the lush, the liveliness and excitement of summer disappears as it flows into and merges with the more contemplative mood of early winter.

In monasteries, as in ordinary farms and households, there is a new round of seasonal activities consisting mostly of the harvest and the early preparations for winter. There are bushels and bushels of new potatoes, squash, onions, and apples to be stored away safely for winter consumption. There is the endless amount of canning, preserving, and freezing of the vegetables and fruits of the harvest. Here in La Grangeville, I prepare a certain amount of tomato sauce to carry us through the cold months. Then follows the harvesting and drying of the herbs that will be used in the kitchen, in our vinegar production to be sold in our small monastic shop. Those of us who are dedicated to the work of the land and live by the immutable rhythms of nature's clock are obliged during the fall months to set aside other occupations and concentrate wholly on the demanding work of the harvest.

The work of the garden also continues, though at a lesser pace than that of the summer months. The fall is usually the best time to divide and transplant the perennials. Then there are the many plants that must be brought inside into the greenhouses so they can survive for the following year. There are also some summer flowering plants that carry on well into autumn and there are those proper to the season which need that first touch of cold before they begin to bloom. The small clematis paniculata, for instance, is one of them. Then there are others like the chrysanthemum, which has become almost a symbol of the season, and the lovely asters which are found not only in the well-ordered garden but also in the fields and the roadsides. Their range of colors—white, deep purple, apricot, pink, and glowing reds—harmonize gloriously with the radiant colors of the trees and the soothing green of the fields.

The liturgy, too, has its own rhythm of feasts and celebrations which in the Northern Hemisphere are closely connected with autumn. The first two feasts perhaps can be most accurately described as late summer feasts because they fall before September 21. However, they look toward winter celebrations and so are naturally associated with autumn. The first of these, the Nativity of Our Lady, is celebrated on September 8. In the Eastern Church, the yearly liturgical cycle begins appropriately on the feast of Mary's birthday, for as one of the texts of the feast explains, this feast announces and forecasts the coming of Christ into this world. The second feast, on September 14, is that of the Exaltation of the Holy Cross. On that day, the winter monastic schedule begins, which includes the monastic fast that, except for Sundays and feast days, will last through Easter. During this time, monks keep the venerable old tradition of cutting down on the amount of food eaten. The fasting increases and becomes stricter during Advent and Lent. On fast days, there is usually one main or complete meal at noontime, and a simple collation of soup, bread, and fruit for supper.

In monastic life, fasting is not viewed only as a form of sacrifice or penance but, more importantly, as a way of bringing under control, thus balancing, the spiritual and the natural in all of us. Fasting also helps to remind us that there are many of our brothers and sisters throughout the world that go to bed hungry every night. We must learn to consume less, so that others may have more to eat.

On September 29, the liturgy invites us to celebrate the memory of the three Holy Archangels: Michael, Gabriel, and Raphael. According to biblical tradition, angels are pure spirits made to adore God and to reflect his infinite divine beauty As messengers of God and our protectors, they minister to us with steadfastness and loving compassion.

October 4 is the feast day of Saint Francis of Assisi, the patron saint of environmentalists. Francis was born in the twelfth century and, after a dramatic con-version, chose to be God's troubadour and sang his heart out for joy all his life long. Love, peace, joy, poverty, and service were the themes of his life. His rever-ence for God was shown in his reverence for all God's creation.

On November 1, we celebrate the feast of All Saints, "la Tousaint" as it is called in France. This is the feast of the family of saints, the friends of God. This feast celebrates the memory not only of canonized saints, but of all those who, glorified by God, are already with Him. On November 2, the liturgy brings to our awareness the memory of the faithful departed. On this day we keep a prayerful and loving remembrance of those among our loved ones who have preceded us to God's kingdom. On this day, it is a custom in France and many other countries to visit the graves of family members and to pray for them. People decorate the tombs with lights and lanterns as a symbol of a love that reaches beyond the reality of death, and they cover the graves of their loved ones with flowers.

During the month of November, another intimate celebration, at least in French monasteries, is the feast of Saint Martin of Tours on November 11, Saint Martin, an early monk and bishop, spent his life in evangelizing France, and as such be was later made one of the patron saints of the country. After the feast of Saint Martin, we move on to the annual celebration of Thanksgiving. When the pilgrims first landed in America they wanted to show their gratitude to God for the happy results of the harvest and so they instituted the custom of giving thanks to the Lord at the end of the harvest season. This has become the national celebration of Thanksgiving Day, when families and friends get together for the traditional elabo-rate dinner in which the abundance of the harvest is well displayed. Both Christian and Jewish communities hold Thanksgiving services, thus providing an occasion to thank the Lord for all his blessings. With Thanksgiving Day we reach somehow the peak of our autumnal celebrations After that there is a steady decline of the season as it gradually seeks to merge with the fast arriving early winter.

"Life starts all over again when it gets crisp in the fall," said F. Scott Fitzgerald. The fall season allows us to see our lives reflected in the beauty of the land all around us: the rolling hills, the harvested fields, the sturdy trees and the thrill of their colors, the harvest moon, the intoxicating chill in the morning air, the farm animals as they seek shelter from the cold. As the trees let go of their leaves, so we, too, must let go of our encumbrances. And as we let go of *all* that is superfluous and unnecessary in our lives, we receive the gift of inner peace. Ultimately, this is autumn's greatest gift to us.

SOUPS AND
APPETIZERS

Harvest Bean Soup
SOUPE AUX HARICOTS

6 servings

1 lb dried white beans
10 cups water
2 onions
3 carrots
3 leeks
1 small turnip
a few leaves of garden greens (spinach or chard, or any other greens)
4 garlic cloves
6 Tbsps olive oil
2 vegetable bouillon cubes
salt and pepper to taste
3 Tbsps fresh parsley, finely chopped

1. Soak the dry beans in cold water for at least five hours, then rinse them well and place them in a large soup pot with the water.

2. Cut thinly the onions, carrots, leeks, turnip, garden greens, and mince the garlic well. Add all this to the soup; also add the olive oil and bouillon cubes.

3. Cook the soup over a medium heat for about 60 minutes, stirring from time to time. Simmer for about 10 minutes more.

4. Add salt and pepper according to taste, and the parsley. Cook for another 5 minutes and serve hot.

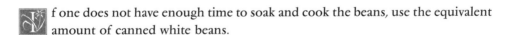 f one does not have enough time to soak and cook the beans, use the equivalent amount of canned white beans.

Rustic Soup
Soupe Rustique

6-8 servings

4 qts water
1 small cabbage
12 Swiss chard leaves (or spinach or escarole)
2 potatoes, peeled and diced
3 carrots, sliced
1 large onion (or 3 leeks)
1 stalk of celery
1/2 cup of small dried beans, soaked overnight
     (black beans, or green beans, such as flageolets)
1/2 cup parsley, minced
1 vegetable bouillon cube
6 Tbsps olive oil
salt and pepper to taste

1. Pour the water into a large saucepan. Cut and thinly slice all the vegetables and add them to the water. Also add the dried beans.

2. When it begins to boil, add the parsley, bouillon cube, and olive oil. Lower the flame to medium heat and cook the soup slowly for about 90 minutes, stirring from time to time and adding more water if it needs it.

3. Add salt and pepper. Simmer for about 10 minutes and serve very hot.

his delicious hearty soup is often made in monasteries and French country homes during harvesttime, thus utilizing the fresh produce of the garden. It is usually made in large quantities, so it can be reheated and used for several days, when the country folk would say it tastes even better.

TARRAGON-PUMPKIN SOUP
POTAGE AU POTIRON

6 servings

10 cups of water
4 cups pumpkin, cubed
3 potatoes, peeled and cubed
2 large carrots, thinly sliced
1 onion, thinly sliced
2 garlic cloves, minced
1 tsp dried tarragon
salt and pepper to taste
1 qt whole milk
1/2 cup vegetable oil
1/2 cup fresh parsley, finely chopped

1. In a large pot bring the water to a boil; then add the pumpkin, potatoes, and carrots. Add the onion, garlic, tarragon, salt, and pepper. Continue to boil for 20 minutes. Reduce heat and simmer for another 20 minutes.

2. Pass the soup through a blender until smooth and creamy and then pour it back into the pot. Add the milk and oil, stir well. Over low heat bring the soup to a boil again. Simmer for about 10 minutes and serve immediately in well-heated soup plates or bowls, garnishing each plate with a pinch of parsley.

umpkin soup is a rather common winter dish in France, certainly more so than in the United States, where people seem to prefer pumpkin pie to pumpkin soup. This particular and appetizing monastic recipe is one of the many variations on the classic French recipe. Those who are concerned about the extra calories in the milk can easily substitute low-fat milk.

I am God's wheat; may I be ground by the teeth of wild beasts that I may become a pure Bread of Christ.

SAINT IGNATIUS OF ANTIOCH

Soup From the Auvergne
POTAGE AUVERGNAT

4 servings

1 cup dried white lima beans (soaked overnight)
8 cups water
1 large carrot, thinly sliced
3 stalks celery, thinly sliced
2 leeks, sliced
2 potatoes, diced
4 garlic cloves, minced
2 fresh sweet peppers, red or green, diced
1 onion, sliced
1 small squash or part of a small pumpkin, cubed
1 bay leaf
pinch of thyme
pinch of fresh parsley
8 Tbsps olive oil
salt and pepper to taste

1. Wash and rinse the previously soaked beans and place them in a casserole filled with 8 cups of water. Add the sliced carrot, celery, leeks, and potatoes. Let them boil for about 20 minutes over a medium-low flame.

2. Then add the minced garlic, peppers, and onion, thinly cut. Peel and cut the squash in cubes, adding it to the soup together with the bay leaf, a pinch of thyme, and freshly minced parsley. Add also the olive oil, salt, and pepper.

3. Allow the soup to simmer for 30 minutes. Remove the bay leaf and serve while still hot.

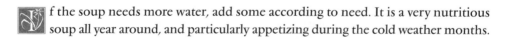 f the soup needs more water, add some according to need. It is a very nutritious soup all year around, and particularly appetizing during the cold weather months.

Garlic Bouillon With Poached Eggs
Aïgo-bouïdo aux oeufs poches

4 servings

> **3 leeks (white part only)**
> **1 onion**
> **2 tomatoes**
> **6 cloves garlic**
> **5 medium-sized potatoes**
> **8 Tbsps olive oil**
> **6 cups water**
> **1 bouquet garni**
> **peel from one orange**
> **pinch of saffron (optional)**
> **salt and pepper**
> **4 eggs**
> **4 slices of French bread**
> **fresh parsley, finely minced**

1. Prepare the bouquet garni by tying together with a thin thread the leaves or sprigs of different herbs (bay leaf, thyme, basil leaves, parsley, and rosemary).

2. Thinly slice the leeks and onion. Peel and grind the tomatoes, discarding the seeds. Peel and mince the garlic. Peel and finely chop the potatoes.

3. In a large saucepan, sauté in olive oil the leeks, onion, and garlic. Add the water, potatoes, bouquet garni, orange peel, saffron, salt, and pepper. Let it boil for about 60 minutes. Then cover with the lid and let it simmer for another 15 minutes. Remove the bouquet garni.

4. While the soup is simmering, poach 4 eggs in the broth for about 3 minutes.

5. Prepare 4 soup dishes, placing a slice of French bread in the center of each. Sprinkle the bread with finely minced parsley. Ladle the soup into each dish and place a poached egg on top of the bread. Sprinkle some finely minced parsley and serve hot.

The Provençal *aïgo-bouïdo* means simply boiled water. It is a rich and hearty dish, either in the fall or in the depth of winter. In the south of France, children learn to love it from their early years and many a mother gives it to her children while they are recovering from a cold.

Saint Geneviève's Soup

SOUPE SAINTE-GENEVIÈVE

4-8 servings

2 medium-sized beets
1 medium-sized turnip
2 carrots
1 large onion
2 potatoes
1 medium-sized bunch of fresh spinach
1 stalk of celery
8 to 10 cups water
1 vegetable bouillon cube
4 Tbsps oil
6 Tbsps fresh parsley, finely chopped
salt and pepper

1. Wash and peel all vegetables. Slice them in small dice. The onion and the spinach should be chopped coarsely.

2. Place the vegetables (except for the parsley) in a large soup pot. Add 8 to 10 cups of water, depending on how thick one would like the soup to be. Bring the water to a boil, then lower to medium heat and continue cooking for about 1 hour. At this point, add the bouillon cube, oil, parsley, salt, and pepper. Stir the soup and let it simmer for 15 minutes. Serve hot.

hough this is basically a good soup for cold weather time, it can be equally satisfying in summertime. Simply pour the soup into a blender and puree thoroughly. Place in the refrigerator for about 2 hours or more, and serve chilled. This soup is named after Saint Geneviève, the patroness of Paris. When she was fifteen years old, she moved to Paris and consecrated herself to God, receiving the veil of a dedicated virgin. She was a visionary and a prophetess, and helped feed the people of Paris in time of famine. She died in the year 500 and her feast is celebrated on January 3.

EGGPLANT AND TOMATO MÉLANGE
RATATOUILLE PROVENÇALE

4 servings

> 3 medium-sized eggplants
> 2 onions
> 1/2 cup olive oil
> 4 tomatoes, peeled and crushed
> 4 zucchini, sliced
> 2 peppers, sliced (one red, one green)
> 2 cloves of garlic, minced
> bouquet garni
> 1 cup pitted black olives
> salt and pepper to taste
> pinch of powdered saffron

1. Prepare the bouquet garni by tying together with a thin thread the leaves or sprigs of different herbs (bay leaf, thyme, basil leaves, parsley, and rosemary).

2. Slice the eggplants and sprinkle them with salt. Set them aside for 20 minutes. Then rinse in cold water.

3. Thinly cut the onions and sauté them in olive oil in a large heavy skillet.

4. Add the tomatoes and the sliced eggplants to the skillet.

5. Cover the skillet and cook for about 5 minutes.

6. Add the zucchini, peppers, garlic, bouquet garni, pitted olives, salt, and pepper.

7. Cover the skillet again and cook slowly for about 30 minutes, until the liquid evaporates. Discard the bouquet garni and serve hot.

CHICKPEA PUREE WITH LEMON
PURÉE DE POIS CHICHES AU CITRON

4-6 servings

10 cups precooked chickpeas
1 lemon
6 Tbsps olive oil
3 garlic cloves, minced
4 Tbsps parsley, finely chopped
salt and pepper to taste
a few black olives, pitted
paprika

1. Place the chickpeas in the blender. Add the juice from one lemon, olive oil, and the finely minced garlic cloves. Blend thoroughly into a purée.

2. Place the purée in a bowl, add the chopped parsley, salt and pepper, and mix by hand with a spoon.

3. Place the purée in a serving dish. Sprinkle paprika over it and spread pitted black olives on top. As garnish, slice tomatoes, a cucumber, and lemon, and place the slices all around the side of the purée.

The chickpea purée can be served warm to accompany the main dish, or it may be served cold as an appetizer, with the tomato and cucumber slices as garnish. Canned drained and rinsed chickpeas may be substituted for the dried chickpeas.

Guard the ground well, for it belongs to God;
Root out the hateful and the bitter weed,
And from the harvest of thy Heart's good seed
The hungry shall be fed, the naked clad,
And love's infection, leaven-like, shall spread
till all creation feeds from heavenly bread.

KENNETH BOULDING

The primeval foods became the earliest culinary comforts of primitive peoples. Soup brewed in caves and grains ground on stones and baked between glowing coals became the sustenance from which early civilization flowed. As long ago as yesterday and as near as tomorrow, bread and soup still sustain and comfort us. Here are our primary nutrients contained in golden loaves. Little wonder bread is called the staff of life...the representation of the body of Christ. For bread is good...as Life is good...as health is good. And soup is a simmering secret of vitamins and minerals ready to nourish us and send us forth. It is probably safe to say that as soon as man (or was it woman?) invented the kettle, he or she promptly invented soup. For what easier, more delectable meal could primitive gourmets concoct than a simmering cauldron of bones and bits of meats, berries, and fruits, served with an elemental bread of ground wild grain mixed with water and baked on a hot, flat stone?

YVONNE YOUNG TARR
THE NEW YORK TIMES BREAD AND SOUP COOKBOOK

MAIN
DISHES

LENTIL MOUSSAKA
MOUSSAKA DE LENTILLES

6 servings

For the lentils:
  2 cups lentils
  olive oil
  3 cloves garlic, minced
  1 large onion, finely chopped
  1 cup mushrooms, chopped
  8 ozs tomato sauce
  2 Tbsps dried oregano
  pinch of thyme
  salt and pepper to taste
  2 medium-sized eggplants, sliced
  3 large tomatoes, sliced

For the sauce:
  2 Tbsps cornstarch or all-purpose flour
  1 1/2 cups milk
  2 Tbsps oil or butter
  1 large egg
  grated cheese (your favorite)
  salt and pepper to taste

1. Boil the lentils for about 5 minutes and then cover the pot and let them simmer for about 30 minutes until tender. Then drain.

2. Pour 8 to 10 tablespoons olive oil into a large frying pan and fry the garlic and onion for a few seconds, stirring constantly so the garlic doesn't burn. Add the mushrooms and lentils and continue cooking for a few minutes, stirring and mixing the ingredients very well. Pour the contents of the frying pan into a large bowl, add the can of tomato sauce, oregano, thyme, salt, and pepper. Mix all ingredients thoroughly.

3. Pour some more olive oil into the frying pan and fry the eggplant slices for 4 minutes, turning them over often. Do not let them burn. Remove the eggplant from the pan and let them cool on a large plate.

4. Grease a deep baking dish and layer the lentil mixture, the eggplants, and the sliced tomatoes. Repeat the layers a second time.

5. To prepare the sauce, dilute 2 tablespoons of cornstarch into 2/3 cup of milk and mix thoroughly. Place this mixture in a saucepan. Add oil, salt, and pepper and start cooking over low heat. Add the rest of the milk slowly and stir continuously until the sauce thickens. Cool it for a few minutes. Beat the egg and mix it well with the white sauce. Pour the sauce over the top of the casserole and then cover it with the grated cheese. Bake for about 45 minutes at 350° F, until the top turns golden brown. Serve steaming hot.

This is a vegetarian version of the classical Greek dish. Besides being nutritious and very delicious, it is also highly economical. Sometimes it is served on feast days at the monastic table.

BASQUE PIPERADE
PIPERADE BASQUE

4 servings

6 Tbsps olive oil
2 onions, sliced
3 peppers, (green, red) sliced
3 tomatoes, peeled and sliced
salt and pepper to taste
1 branch thyme
1 branch basil
6 eggs
1/2 cup of Bayonne ham, diced small (optional)

1. Pour the olive oil in a large skillet and cook the sliced onions and peppers over medium heat until they turn golden. Add the peeled tomatoes, salt, and pepper, and a bouquet of thyme and basil (tied with a thin thread). Cook it slowly until the liquid evaporates.

2. In the meantime, in a large bowl, beat well six eggs.

3. Remove the branches of thyme and basil from the vegetables. Pour the egg mixture over the top of the cooked vegetables and stir continually over medium-low heat until it sets. Be careful not to overcook. Serve immediately while it is still hot.

 quick and appetizing dish for a Sunday brunch. Nonvegetarians may add slices of Bayonne ham for extra substance.

> *As a careful cultivation of land first turns the soil, and cleanses it from weeds and thistles, and afterward casts the seed; so one who expects to receive from God the seed of grace, must first cleanse the soil of the heart, that the seed of the Spirit falling therein may bring forth perfect and abundant faith.*
>
> SAINT MACARIUS, PATRON OF PASTRY CHEFS

POTATO SOUFFLÉ
SOUFFLÉ DE POMMES DE TERRE

4-6 servings

1/2 lb potatoes
1 cup milk
4 Tbsps butter
salt and pepper to taste
5 eggs, separated
10 Tbsps heavy cream or crème fraîche (see page 213)
1/3 cup grated cheese (your favorite)
pinch of freshly grated nutmeg (optional)

1. Wash and peel the potatoes. Boil them for about 20 minutes. When the potatoes are cooked, drain them thoroughly and mash them to a purée.

2. Pour the milk into a casserole dish, add the potato purée, butter, salt, and pepper, and mix gently over low heat, stirring constantly. Withdraw from the heat and let it cool.

3. In a bowl, beat the egg yolks and the crème fraîche together. Add the grated cheese and mix well. Place the potato purée into the bowl and blend all ingredients thoroughly.

4. With an electric mixer beat the egg whites separately until they become firm. Delicately fold the egg whites little by little into the potato mixture.

5. Butter well a soufflé dish. Sprinkle some extra grated cheese over the butter and carefully place the potato-egg mixture into the dish. Bake in a preheated oven at 350° F for about 20 to 25 minutes. When the soufflé is ready, serve immediately.

The monk finally seeks solitude and silence...because he knows that the real fruit of his vocation is union with God in love and contemplation. An apt saying of the Moslem Sufis comes to mind here: The hen does not lay eggs in the market place.

THOMAS MERTON

SCRAMBLED EGGS WITH EGGPLANT
OEUFS BROUILLÉS AUX AUBERGINES

4 servings

1 eggplant
1 onion
2 Tbsps butter
pinch of paprika
6 eggs
1/2 cup heavy cream
4 slices of bread
salt and pepper to taste

1. Cut the eggplant in cubes and slice the onion very thin. In a large frying pan sauté both in butter for about 6 to 8 minutes. Add the paprika and turn constantly.

2. In a large bowl, beat the eggs well. Add the heavy cream, salt, and pepper, and beat slowly either with a mixer or by hand. Pour over the eggplant in the frying pan and cook over medium heat, stirring often. Remove from heat when the eggs begin to set but are still moist.

3. Serve it hot over the top of a toasted slice of bread.

My children, your heart is small, but prayer enlarges it and makes it capable of loving God. Prayer is a foretaste of heaven, a passing glimpse into paradise. It never leaves us without sweetness. It is a honey which comes down into the soul and sweetens everything. Sorrow melts away before a well-offered prayer, like snow before the sun.

SAINT JOHN VIANNEY

SPAGHETTI WITH GREEN SAUCE
SPAGHETTI SAUCE VERTE

4 servings

3 qts water
1/2 lb thin spaghetti noodles
1/2 cup olive oil
8 garlic cloves, finely minced
1 bunch fresh parsley, finely cut and minced
salt and pepper to taste
grated Romano or Parmesan cheese

1. Pour the water into a large pot and bring to a boil. Add the spaghetti, stirring continually. Add salt and cook the noodles for about 5 minutes, seeing that they remain *al dente*.

2. While the spaghetti is boiling, pour the olive oil into another pan and add the minced garlic, stirring continually over low heat so it doesn't burn. Add the parsley and fresh pepper and continue to cook for a few seconds. Pass through the blender until smooth.

3. Pour the garlic-parsley sauce over the drained spaghetti. Mix thoroughly. Sprinkle some grated cheese on top and serve hot.

White Tuna and Potatoes Saint Guenole

Thon aux pommes de terre Saint-Guénolé

6-8 servings

For the tuna:
- 4 Tbsps butter
- 3 lbs white tuna
- bouquet garni
- 1 large onion, chopped
- salt and pepper

For the potatoes:
- 3 lbs potatoes
- 4 Tbsps butter
- 2 cups whole milk
- salt to taste

1. Prepare the bouquet garni by tying together with a thin thread the leaves or sprigs of different herbs (bay leaf, thyme, basil leaves, parsley, and rosemary).

2. Melt the butter in a frying pan. Add the tuna and sauté slowly over medium-low heat without allowing the butter to burn. Stir steadily.

3. Chop the onion and add to the tuna. Add the bouquet garni, salt, and pepper, and stir a few times. When the onion begins to turn golden, turn off the heat. Cover the pan and let it sit for 20 minutes. Remove the bouquet garni.

4. Boil the potatoes until they are cooked. Mash them into a purée, adding the butter, milk, and salt. Serve a portion of tuna and a portion of the potatoes on the side.

his recipe is of Breton origin, that is to say, it comes from Brittany, a region that is in itself a world apart. The people from Brittany, of Celtic Gallic origin, are one of those groups in France who never totally succumbed to the Latin-Roman civilization brought by outside invaders. They were able to retain their ancient language and culture. Because of Brittany's geographical location near the Atlantic Ocean, seafood is one of the important elements of the Breton table. Saint Guenole was a holy monk of the region who founded a monastery in 485.

The monastery survived, as did most French monasteries, until the French revolution, when the monks were dispersed. It was restored again in 1958 by the monks of nearby Kerbeneat. Today as in the past, the Abbey of Landevennec is a center of prayer, liturgy, and culture for the people of Brittany and all those who come to it. In 1985, the abbey celebrated the fifteen-hundredth anniversary of its foundation.

For prayer and a melody every hour is suitable,
that while one's hands are busy with their tasks
we may praise God with the tongue, or, if not, with
the heart.

SAINT BASIL

EGGS SAINT ODILE
OEUFS SAINTE-ODILE

4 servings

6 ripe and good-sized tomatoes
1 large onion, minced
4 garlic cloves, minced
4 Tbsps olive oil
1/3 cup dry white wine
pinch of cayenne pepper
salt to taste
herbs: parsley, basil, thyme (optional)
4 eggs

1. Boil the tomatoes whole for a few minutes. Rinse them in cold water, peel them, and then cut each in 4 even quarters. Slice and mince both the onion and garlic. Mix the tomatoes, onion, and garlic in a deep bowl.

2. Pour the olive oil into a large frying pan and add the vegetables from the bowl. Cover the pan and let it cook over medium heat for about 5 minutes. Stir, then add the wine, cayenne pepper, salt, and herbs to the frying pan, stirring from time to time until it achieves the good consistency of a sauce.

3. Thoroughly butter 4 small individual baking dishes such as those used to serve French onion soup. Pour the sauce equally into the 4 dishes. Break the eggs and place one at the center of each dish. Sprinkle some salt and a pinch of cayenne on the top of each egg. Bake in a preheated oven at 300° F for about 15 minutes. The egg whites must be thoroughly cooked but the yolks should remain mellow and slightly juicy as with fried eggs. Serve hot, straight out of the oven.

This recipe is one of the many variations of a dish rather common throughout France and Spain. Some people use wine in the sauce and others don't. Some prefer black pepper to cayenne and others do not. Some prefer cooking the eggs right in the frying pan rather than in the oven. In any case, it is a basically simple recipe and, for Americans, a welcome variation from the rather routine way of preparing and serving eggs in this country.

RICE PILAF
RIZ PILAF

6 servings

6 Tbsps olive oil
1 large onion, well chopped
2 cups long-grain rice
8 mushrooms, finely chopped
5 cups water, boiling
1 vegetable bouillon cube
1 bay leaf
pinch of thyme
salt and pepper to taste

1. Pour the olive oil into a large saucepan and fry the onion and rice for a minute or two. Stir continually.

2. Add the water, mushrooms, bouillon cube, bay leaf, thyme, salt, and pepper. Stir well and cook over low heat, until all the liquid is absorbed and the rice is done. Serve hot. Remove the bay leaf before serving.

This simple and tasty rice dish is a good accompaniment to seafood and egg dishes, and it is a welcome variation on the usual plain rice.

We may live without poetry, music and art;
We may live without conscience, and live without heart;
We may live without friends; we may live without books;
But civilized man cannot live without cooks.

EDWARD ROBERT BULWER
1ST EARL OF LYTTON

FILLET OF SOLE ALSATIAN STYLE
FILET DE SOLE À L'ALSACIENNE

6 servings

6 fillets of sole
4 shallots, finely minced
4 Tbsps fresh parsley, minced
1 cup white Alsatian wine
salt and pepper to taste
1/2 cup heavy cream
3 Tbsps butter or margarine
2/3 cup seedless grapes

1. Clean and wipe the fillets with a cloth or paper towel. Thoroughly butter a long flat baking dish and cover the bottom of the dish with the minced shallots and the chopped parsley.

2. Place the fillets on top of the shallots and parsley. Pour the wine all around the fillets. (Use more wine if necessary.) Sprinkle salt and pepper on the fillets. Bake covered at 350° F for 15 to 20 minutes.

3. Drain the fish, pouring the juice into a small casserole. Place the fish in the oven to keep it warm. Add the heavy cream and butter to the casserole and cook over medium-low heat while stirring often. When the sauce is done, pour over the fillets and sprinkle the seedless grapes on the top. Serve hot.

Hospitality consists in a little fire,
a little food,
and an immense quiet.
RALPH WALDO EMERSON

SAINT BERTILLE TAGLIATELLES
TAGLIATELLES DE LA SAINTE BERTILLE

4-6 servings

3/4 cup walnuts, chopped
1 cup half-and-half cream
10 ozs goat cheese, crumbled
pinch of nutmeg
pinch of black pepper
12 ozs tagliatelle noodles (or egg noodles)
salt to taste
3 parsley sprigs (leaf and stem), finely chopped
grated Romano cheese, as needed

1. Place the walnuts in a heavy cast-iron skillet and heat them over a low-medium flame. Toast and stir continually for 2 to 3 minutes. Set aside.

2. Pour the half-and-half into a small casserole, heat over a low-medium flame. Add the goat cheese, nutmeg, and pepper. Stir continually until it reaches a rich creamy consistency. Turn off the heat and cover the casserole. Keep it hot.

3. In the meantime, cook the tagliatelle noodles in boiling, salted water for about 5 to 6 minutes. Do not overcook, for the noodles must be *al dente*. When they are cooked, drain them.

4. Place the cooked noodles in a large pasta bowl, add parsley and pour the sauce over them and toss. Cover the top with the chopped walnuts and the grated cheese. Serve at once.

Saint Bertille was born in northern France. Encouraged by Saint Ouen, the bishop of Rouen, she embraced monastic life at the abbey of Jourarre, near Meaux. Later on, when the nearby abbey of Chelles was refounded, she was sent with a small group of nuns from Jouarre to form the new community and she was named the first Abbess. Her reputation as a saintly nun and the monastic discipline she established at Chelles attracted many vocations, including foreign ones. She died beloved by all. Her feast is kept on November 5.

CELERY WITH MORNAY SAUCE
CÉLERIS À LA MORNAY

4 servings

> **1 bunch of celery**
> **1 onion, sliced and finely chopped**
> **2 cups Mornay sauce (see page 206)**
> **1/3 cup breadcrumbs**
> **1/2 cup grated cheese (preferably Gruyère)**
> **4 Tbsps butter**
> **salt to taste**

1. Choose a fresh and good-sized head of celery. Wash and trim the bottom and the leaves on the top. Slice the celery into bite-size pieces. Cook in salty boiling water until tender. Drain thoroughly and mix with the chopped onion.

2. Prepare a Mornay sauce. (For more flavor in the Mornay sauce, add some extra grated cheese.)

3. Butter thoroughly a 2" deep baking dish. Cover the bottom of the dish with part of the Mornay sauce. Place the celery-onion mixture on top of the sauce. Sprinkle the grated cheese on top of the celery and cover the entire surface with the rest of the Mornay sauce. Sprinkle the breadcrumbs on top of the sauce and small pieces of butter over the crumbs. Place the dish in a 300° F oven for at least 20 to 25 minutes until the top is brown. Serve hot.

> *When humility delivers us from attachment to our own works and our own reputation, we discover that perfect joy is only possible when we have completely forgotten ourselves. And it is only when we pay no more attention to our own life and our own reputation and our own excellence that we are at least completely free to serve God in perfection for God's own sake alone.*
>
> THOMAS MERTON

POTATO PANCAKES FROM BAYONNE
CRÊPES DE POMMES DE TERRE À LA BAYONNAISE

4-6 servings

2 cups raw grated potatoes
3 eggs
6 Tbsps flour
2/3 cup whole milk
1 tsp salt
pinch of baking powder
1/4 cup scallions, finely chopped
1/4 cup parsley, finely chopped
oil or butter for cooking

1. Wash, clean, and dry the potatoes. Grate the potatoes to fill two cups.

2. Beat the eggs in a deep bowl, adding the flour, milk, salt, and baking powder. Blend thoroughly with a mixer. Then add the potatoes, scallions, and parsley, and stir the batter by hand. Refrigerate the batter for 1 hour.

3. With a small ladle, drop the batter into a well-greased, preheated crêpe pan and tilt to cover the whole bottom of the skillet. Cook until it begins to brown and immediately turn over with a spatula and cook the other side. Use a small crêpe pan so that they are not too large in size. They are more attractive when they are thin and small in size.

There are enormous amounts of regional varieties of crêpes throughout France. This particular one comes to us from Bayonne, an important center in the Basque country and part of the ancient lands of Guyenne-Aquitaine that has quite a remarkable history of its own. Since this corner of France is basically maritime and they live out of the abundance of the sea, these potato pancakes are usually served to accompany seafood. However, they can accompany any egg or meat dish, and they are delicious simply on their own.

Your strength will be in silence and hope.
RULE OF CARMEL

Peppers and Eggplant Italian Style

POIVRONNADE À L'ITALIENNE

4 servings

3 eggplants
3 peppers (red, green, yellow)
1 large onion
3 tomatoes, peeled
3 celery stalks
8 Tbsps olive oil
4-oz jar green pitted olives
salt and pepper to taste
basil and thyme (optional)

1. Cut the eggplants into cubes and place them in a deep dish. Sprinkle some salt and mix. Let it rest for about 30 minutes. Thoroughly rinse and drain.

2. Cut the peppers and onion in thin circles. Slice also the tomatoes and celery.

3. Pour the olive oil into a large pan, add the onion, and cook it slowly until it begins to turn brown. Add the eggplants, peppers, celery, and tomatoes. Let it cook slowly over medium low heat for about 30 minutes. Cover the pan, but stir its contents from time to time. Towards the end, add the well-rinsed olives, salt, and pepper. Continue cooking for 5 extra minutes; then let it simmer for another 5 minutes. Serve it hot.

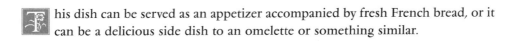

his dish can be served as an appetizer accompanied by fresh French bread, or it can be a delicious side dish to an omelette or something similar.

...When through love the soul goes beyond all working of the intellect and all images in the mind and is rapt above itself, utterly leaving itself, it flows into God: then is God its peace and fullness. It loses itself in the infinite solitude and darkness of the Godhead; but so to lose itself is rather to find itself. The soul is, as it were, all God-colored, because its essence is bathed in the Essence of God.

LOUIS DE BLOIS

SAINT PACHOMIUS PUMPKIN BEIGNETS
BEIGNETS DE POTIRON SAINT PACHÔME

6 servings

1 lb pumpkin, cut in quarters and peeled
4 egg whites, beaten stiff
1 Tbsp flour
4 ozs grated Parmesan cheese
pinch of nutmeg
pinch of paprika
salt and pepper to taste
vegetable or olive oil, as needed, for frying

1. Slice the pumpkin in cubes. Place them in a blender and whirl them.

2. In a deep bowl beat the egg whites until stiff. Add the flour, cheese, nutmeg, paprika, salt, and pepper; beat some more until all ingredients are well blended. Add the pumpkin and mix well with the help of a fork.

3. Heat the oil in a large skillet, fill a serving spoon with the mixture, then plunge it into the hot oil. When one side is done, turn it over. Do two or three at a time. When they are done, place the beignets on a paper towel to absorb the oil. Serve them warm.

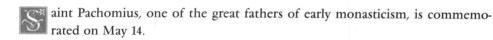 aint Pachomius, one of the great fathers of early monasticism, is commemorated on May 14.

Green String Beans Spanish Style
HARICOTS VERTS À L'ESPAGNOLE

4 servings

1 lb green string beans
salt to taste
4 garlic cloves
6 Tbsps olive oil
pepper to taste

1. Wash the beans well, trim the ends, and cut them in half. Boil them for about 15 minutes without covering the saucepan. Add salt at the end.

2. Peel and mince the garlic. Place it in a saucepan with the olive oil and sauté over low heat for 1 minute. Rinse the beans well and place them gently into the oil. Continue to sauté for another minute or two while adding some pepper to it. Serve it hot.

Carrot Puree
PURÉE DE CAROTTES

6 servings

10 large carrots
4 cups water
salt to taste (no more than 1/2 teaspoon in any case!)
5 Tbsps brown sugar
6 Tbsps heavy cream
4 Tbsps butter, melted

1. Wash and peel the carrots and boil them in water. When the carrots are tender, add the salt. Pour the carrots and their juice—no more than two cups—into a blender and thoroughly blend the mixture into a purée.

2. Pour the purée into a bowl, adding the sugar, heavy cream, and melted butter, and mix very well. Pour the purée into a buttered baking dish. (If necessary, add more brown sugar according to taste.) Bake in the oven at 350° F for about 30 minutes. Serve hot. (Or, during the summer, instead of the oven, put it in the refrigerator for 2 hours and serve it cold.)

SALADS

SAINT HILDEGARD'S SALAD

SALADE SAINTE-HILDEGARDE

6 servings

> **1/2 lb Belgian endives**
> **1/2 lb Swiss cheese**
> **1/3 cup scallions, chopped**
> **1/3 cup mayonnaise (see page 215)**
> **1/4 cup heavy cream (optional)**
> **1 tsp Dijon mustard**
> **2 tsps lemon juice**
> **1 tsp white dry vermouth**

1. Wash and drain the endives. Separate the leaves and cut them into inch-long pieces. Place the endive leaves in a salad bowl.

2. Cut the Swiss cheese into cubes and add to the endives in the bowl. Also add the chopped scallions.

3. In a small bowl, combine the mayonnaise (one can also use the commercial type), heavy cream, mustard, lemon juice, and white vermouth. Using a mixer, beat until stiff. Pour the sauce over the endives, cheese, and scallions. Mix well and set in the refrigerator for at least 1 hour before serving. Serve cold.

Saint Hildegard is considered today one of the most remarkable, creative personalities of the Middle Ages. Hildegard of Bingen was born of noble parents near Alzev, Germany. While still a young child, she was entrusted to the care of Jutta of Spanheim, abbess of a small community of Benedictine nuns. When Jutta died in 1136, Hildegard was elected abbess of the community. She once saw tongues of flame descend from heaven and settle upon her, a sign that foretold the incredible life she would lead as a visionary, naturalist, playwright, poetess, and composer. Both her writings and her songs are among the finest of the Middle Ages. Today she is being discovered not only by monks and nuns but also by large numbers of scholars and students who are fascinated by the legacy of the intense and passionate abbess of Bingen.

SALADE LANDAISE

6 servings

For the salad:
- 2 lbs fresh string beans
- 1 cup croutons
- 1 onion, thinly sliced
- 8 ozs cheese, diced and cubed (any cheese of preference)
- 1 Tbsp parsley, chopped
- 1 Tbsp tarragon, finely minced

For the vinaigrette:
- 1/2 cup olive oil
- 3 Tbsps tarragon vinegar
- 2 Tbsps lemon juice
- salt and pepper to taste

1. Wash and trim the string beans. Cook them uncovered in salty boiling water. The beans must be tender yet remain firm. When the beans are done, rinse them immediately with cold water. This helps them retain their freshness and color. Drain well.

2. While the beans are boiling, prepare the vinaigrette by mixing thoroughly all the ingredients mentioned above.

3. Place the string beans in a salad bowl. Add the croutons, onion, and the vinaigrette, toss the salad. Spread the cheese cubes on top of the salad and sprinkle the finely chopped parsley and tarragon over the salad. This salad can be served lukewarm, or it can be refrigerated and served cold.

This recipe comes to us from the ancient region of Gascony in France. The actual recipe calls for the use of *paté de foie gras de carnard* (liver paté) which creates a wonderful contrast with the French string beans—a contrast worthy of those truly *gourmands*. However, in the monastic setting, we are ruled by simplicity and sobriety and consequently we substitute the delicious paté with small chunks of cheese, which is perhaps healthier and somehow no less appetizing. One sort of cheese that goes well in this particular recipe is one made by the Trappist monks from Gethsemane Abbey in Kentucky. I strongly recommend it.

SAINT FRANCIS SALAD
SALADE SAINT FRANÇOIS

4 servings

4 medium-sized beets
6 medium-sized potatoes
6 Belgian endives
1 medium-sized onion, finely chopped
vinaigrette with mustard (page 214)
fines herbes (tarragon, parsley, chervil, chives, finely chopped)

1. Wash and peel the beets and potatoes. Boil them separately until tender when checked with a fork. Cut them in long, thin slices, as one does for French fries. Place them in a salad bowl. Cut the endives in half and in thin strips lengthwise and add to the salad bowl. Add the finely chopped onion.

2. Prepare the vinaigrette and pour over the salad. Sprinkle the fines herbes and toss the salad lightly before serving.

Saint Francis's feast is celebrated on October 4, during harvesttime. This simple, plain salad is prepared with vegetables that are harvested around that time. Of course, while the fall may be the appropriate time to prepare it, people who love different varieties of salads welcome it at any time of the year.

Throw open wide your senses, longing intensely with each of them for all which is God.

HADEWIJCH OF ANTWERP
TWELFTH CENTURY MYSTIC

SAINT SIMEON SALAD
SALADE SAINT SIMEON

4 servings

4 red, ripe, firm, tomatoes
1 red onion, thinly sliced
16 green olives, pitted
4 mozzarella cheese slices, cut about 1/4-inch thick
a handful of fresh basil leaves, coarsely chopped
salt and freshly ground pepper to taste
extra-virgin olive oil to taste

1. Trim the ends of the tomatoes, then cut them into 1/2-inch thick slices.

2. Arrange the tomato slices in an even circular pattern in four individual serving dishes. Distribute evenly over the tomatoes the thin onion slices. Sprinkle salt and pepper over the top of the tomatoes and onions. Place four olives in each plate. Place one mozzarella slice per dish over the tomatoes at the center. Sprinkle the basil evenly over each plate.

3. Drizzle with olive oil over the entire top and serve immediately after. This is an excellent appetizer to serve when the tomatoes are in season.

The Eagle soars in the summit of Heaven.
The Hunter with his dogs pursues his circuit.
O perpetual revolution of configured stars.
O perpetual recurrence of determined seasons.
O world of spring and autumn, birth and dying!

T. S. ELIOT

SPANISH SALAD
SALADE À L'ESPAGNOLE

6 servings

> **6 ripe tomatoes**
> **4 sweet peppers (2 red and 2 green)**
> **2 cucumbers, peeled**
> **1 large red onion**
> **pitted green olives**
> **oil and vinegar**
> **salt and pepper**

1. Wash and rinse the vegetables. Cut the tomatoes, peppers, and cucumbers in thin even slices.

2. Cut the onion in round thin slices and place them in a bowl of hot water for about 3 or 4 minutes to take the sting away. Rinse thoroughly.

3. Mix all the vegetables in a large salad bowl. Add the olives. Just before serving, prepare a simple vinaigrette (see recipe on page 214), and pour over the salad. Mix well.

This is the perfect sort of salad to have when these vegetables are in season and all through the fall when the last fruits of the garden are being harvested before the first frost arrives.

Practice patience toward everyone, and especially toward yourself. Never be disturbed because of your imperfections, but always get up bravely after a fall.

SAINT FRANCIS DE SALES

SAINT MARTIN'S SALAD

SALADE SAINT-MARTIN

4 servings

For the salad:
  1 avocado
  2 Belgian endives
  1 bunch of watercress
  1 large carrot, grated very fine
  1/2 cup mushrooms, thinly sliced (optional)

For the vinaigrette:
  6 Tbsps olive oil
  2 Tbsps wine vinegar (preferably white wine tarragon vinegar)
  dash of dry mustard
  salt and pepper to taste

1. Peel the avocado and cut it into chunks. Wash and dry all the other vegetables, thoroughly separating the individual endive leaves and the watercress sprigs. Place them in a large bowl. Add the carrot (and optional mushrooms).

2. In a small bowl, prepare the vinaigrette sauce by mixing all the ingredients well. Pour over the salad just before serving, tossing it lightly.

Saint Martin de Tours is one of the great saints of ancient Gaul. The son of a pagan officer, he converted to Christianity after he had a vision of Christ clad in his half cloak, which he had given earlier to a poor beggar. Later on he became a hermit at Ligugé near Poitiers, where he later organized one of the first monastic communities in Gaul. Despite his great objections, he was later named bishop of Tours. When he moved to Tours, he established a monastery at Marmoutier, where he continued leading a monastic life combined with his duties as a bishop. He died in 397 and his tomb in Tours became one of the most celebrated centers of pilgrimages during the Middle Ages. He was one of the earliest pioneers of monasticism in the West, much before Saint Benedict. Today a Benedictine monastic community, established at the very site of Ligugé, carries on the tradition first established there by Saint Martin. He is one of the most beloved saints of France and one of its patron saints. His feast is celebrated on November 11, when there is usually a brief spell of Indian summer, called appropriately in France *l'été de la Saint-Martin*.

DESSERTS

PUMPKIN AND APPLE COMPOTE

COMPOTE DE POTIRON ET DE POMMES

6 servings

5 cups water
1/2 cup sugar
2 Tbsps vanilla extract (or equivalent of your favorite liqueur)
6 large apples, peeled
1 small pumpkin or butternut squash, peeled
1 long lemon peel, minced
pinch of nutmeg and/or a dash of cinnamon (optional)

1. In a large saucepan, bring the water to a boil, with the sugar and vanilla extract. Lower to medium heat. Add the peeled apples and pumpkin cut evenly in small chunks. Add the lemon peel and nutmeg and/or cinnamon, if desired. Cook for about 15 minutes, then simmer for an equal amount of time. Do not let the fruit become too soft or mushy. It should remain rather firm.

2. Let the compote cool at room temperature for about 30 minutes. Serve lukewarm during the cold days or chill for about 1 hour in the refrigerator and serve it cold if the weather is mild.

ompotes of any sort are simple and quickly made desserts and consequently you find them very often in French monasteries. With typical monastic frugality, the monks make compotes out of the last fruits of the season which are beginning to turn after surviving the long winter in the monastery cellar.

The only thing we can offer to God of value is to give our love to people as
unworthy of it as we are of God's love.

SAINT CATHERINE OF SIENA

BANANAS FLAMBÉ
BANANES FLAMBÉES

6 servings

6 bananas
confectioners' sugar
flour
1 egg, beaten
4 Tbsps butter
Grand-Marnier liqueur

1. Choose 6 medium, rather firm bananas and carefully cut them in half lengthwise. Carefully roll them in the confectioners' sugar, then roll them in white flour.

2. Beat the egg in a wide soup dish. Pass each banana through the egg and then delicately roll once more through the flour.

3. Melt butter into a large frying pan and cook the bananas over medium heat. Turn them carefully so they don't fall apart. When they are done, place them with great care in a long serving dish. Sprinkle with more confectioners' sugar and then generously pour the Grand-Marnier over them. Just before serving, flambé them at the table. Eat them immediately after.

When the bananas are cooked and prepared in this fashion, they give a distinctive and delicious aroma. And though this recipe may be simple and quick to prepare, it is nevertheless an elegant dessert to present at the table.

> *I no longer believe that we can change anything*
> *in the world until we have first changed ourselves.*
> ETTY HILLESUM

CLAFOUTIS
CLAFOUTI

6 servings

2 lbs pitted cherries (or 32-oz canned cherries)
1 cup whole milk
4 eggs
1/2 cup granulated sugar
2 tsps vanilla extract
confectioners' sugar

1. Preheat the oven to 350° F. If using canned cherries, drain them thoroughly.

2. Prepare the batter by placing the milk, eggs, sugar, and vanilla extract in the blender and whirl at high speed for a minute or two.

3. Butter thoroughly a square flat baking dish about 2" deep. Pour about one-fourth of the batter into the baking dish and place in the oven for about 2 minutes, until the batter has set at the bottom of the dish. Remove the dish from the oven and spread the cherries evenly over the surface of the batter. One may sprinkle a bit of sugar over the cherries. Then, pour the rest of the batter on top of the cherries, spreading evenly over the entire dish. Place the dish in the center of the oven and bake for about 30 minutes. The clafouti is done when the top puffs and turns brown, though it still remains custard-like.

4. Remove from the oven, sprinkle some confectioners' sugar over the surface, and serve at the table while the clafouti is still warm.

Three enemies of personal peace: regret over yesterday's mistakes, anxiety over tomorrow's problems, and ingratitude for today's blessings.

WILLIAM ARTHUR WARD

APPLES BAKED WITH CIDER
POMMES CUITES AU CIDRE

6 servings

6 large Golden Delicious apples
2 ozs butter
1 cup apple cider
1/3 cup granulated sugar
2 Tbsps heavy cream
freshly ground nutmeg
6 Tbsps blackberry jam

1. Peel and core the apples, leaving them whole.

2. Butter thoroughly a deep baking dish. Pour the cider into the dish and then add the apples. Sprinkle the sugar over the apples and cider. Sprinkle also a pinch of nutmeg on top of each apple. Bake in the oven at 300° F for about 40 minutes.

3. At the end of the baking, take the dish out of the oven and fill the inside of the apples with blackberry jam. Pour a bit of heavy cream on top of each apple and place the dish again in the oven for another 5 minutes. Serve hot.

This is a simple and elegant country dish for the cold evenings of fall and winter. It is also a dessert that takes little time to prepare.

Every day we are changing, every day we are dying,
and yet we fancy ourselves eternal.

SAINT JEROME

SWEET CRÊPES
CRÊPES SUCRÉES

6 servings (about 12 crêpes)

4 eggs
2 Tbsps oil (or 2 Tbsps melted butter)
pinch of salt
3 Tbsps sugar
1 tsp vanilla extract (or Calvados, rum, or any other liqueur)
1 1/4 cups flour
4 cups milk

1. In a large bowl, mix all the ingredients and beat with the mixer, adding one cup of milk at a time. The batter should have the consistency of heavy cream and ought to be free from all flour lumps. If the batter is too thick, add one or two teaspoons of cold water and continue beating until it is light and smooth. Refrigerate the batter for an hour or two before starting to use.

2. Heat a 6" or 8" crêpe skillet over a high flame and grease lightly the entire pan with a bit of oil or melted butter, using one of those very convenient small pastry brushes. Using a small ladle, pour about 3 tablespoons of batter into the skillet and tip it immediately, seeing that the batter covers the entire bottom and quickly becomes firm. Cook the crêpe for about one minute, until it begins to show signs of turning brown around the rim. With a spatula, rapidly turn it over and cook the other side for about one minute or so. When the crêpe is done, gently slide it onto a flat plate. Brush the crêpe skillet once more and continue with the rest of the crêpes.

3. Butter well a large baking dish and carefully place the rolled crêpes one next to the other. Sprinkle some confectioners' sugar or granulated sugar on top of them and bake them for about 15 minutes at 300° F. Before serving, pour some rum over them, and serve them flambée.

This simple basic French recipe can be used with all sorts of fillings, salted or sweet, and when they are served, they give a special touch of charm and warmth at the table.

One pancake for lunch and half a boiled egg for dinner makes a man at sixty able to do anything a college athlete can do.

SIR WILLIAM OSLER

PEARS FROM BURGUNDY
POIRES À LA BOURGUIGNONNE

6 servings

2 lbs small, firm pears
1 1/2 cups sugar
1 tsp cinnamon
1 cup water
1 cup red Burgundy wine

1. Peel the pears but keep them whole. Place them in a saucepan and add the sugar, cinnamon, and water. Cover the pan and bring to a light boil for about 10 minutes. Add the wine and boil lightly for another 5 minutes. Simmer for 15 minutes with the saucepan uncovered.

2. Place the pears in a shallow serving dish. Boil down the juice until it has the consistency of a light syrup (do not overboil). Pour it over the pears and chill. This dessert must be served cold.

This dish is a lovely dessert to serve during the harvest months, with fresh pears from the orchards. It is also a simple and elegant dessert that can be enjoyed all year round.

For a small reward a man will hurry away on a long journey,
while for eternal life many will hardly take a single step.

THOMAS À KEMPIS

RICE TART
TARTE AUX RIZ

6 servings

For the filling:
  1 Tbsp butter
  3/4 cup long-grain rice
  1 qt milk
  2 eggs, separated
  2 tsps vanilla extract
  1/2 cup granulated sugar
  1 Tbsp almond extract

For the pastry shell *(la Pâte Brisée):*
  1 egg
  3 Tbsps granulated sugar
  1 cup all-purpose flour
  1 stick sweet butter or margarine
  5 Tbsps ice water
  pinch of salt

1. Following the instructions for the tart shell on page 222, prepare the dough for the crust the day before and let it stand overnight in the refrigerator until you are ready to use it.

2. Melt the butter in a good-sized saucepan. Add the rice and stir well for one minute or two. Add immediately the milk and cook the rice over low heat, stirring from time to time until all the milk is absorbed and the rice is cooked and tender. Let it cool.

3. Beat the egg yolks, then add the vanilla, sugar, and almond extract, and beat some more. Add the eggs to the rice and mix well. Beat the egg whites stiff and fold carefully into the rice.

4. Preheat the oven at 375° F. Bake the tart shell for about 10 minutes or so until the rim begins to turn golden brown. Pour the rice mixture into the shell and spread evenly. Bake for about 30 minutes until the top reflects a light brown color and the crust is done.

PEAR COMPOTE WITH MERINGUE

COMPOTE DE POIRES MERINGÉE

6 servings

6 pears
6 cups water
1 cup granulated sugar
2 Tbsps lemon juice
1 tsp vanilla extract
pinch of nutmeg
4 egg whites
confectioners' sugar

1. Peel the pears and cut them in halves. Pour water in a saucepan. Add the lemon juice, half a cup of sugar, vanilla, nutmeg, and pears. Boil for about 3 or 4 minutes. The pears must remain firm, so do not overcook them. Keep them in their syrup until ready to use.

2. With a mixer, beat the egg whites, gradually sprinkling in the remaining sugar. In a flat baking dish arrange the pears evenly. Pour a cup and a half of the syrup over the pears. Cover the top of the entire dish with the meringue. Spread evenly with a fork. Sprinkle some confectioners' sugar over the top. Bake at 300⁰ F for about 25 to 30 minutes.

When we feel within ourselves that we desire God, then God has touched the mainspring of power, and through this touch it swings beyond itself and towards God.

THEOLOGIA GERMANICA

FLAN PARIS STYLE
FLAN À LA PARISIENNE

4 servings

1 cup all-purpose flour
1/2 cup sugar
4 eggs
1 oz sweet butter, melted
4 cups milk (mixed with a vanilla bean for a few hours before)
1 Tbsp Napoleon brandy

1. Place the flour in a deep bowl. Make a hollow place in the center and put the sugar into it. Break the eggs into the bowl, add the melted butter and mix thoroughly by hand or with the help of a mixer.

2. Gradually add the milk while continuing the process of mixing until the texture is totally smooth. Add the brandy and mix some more.

3. Butter a flan mold thoroughly and pour the mixture into it. Place the mold into a larger pan containing water so that half the flan mold is immersed in the water to cook *au bain-marie*. Place this into the oven. Bake at 350° F for about 40 minutes. Unmold the flan and place in the refrigerator for at least one hour. Serve cold.

When with the help of God my self is purified,
To go to God I need not wander far and wide.
When all is nothingness to you, when you embrace
Nothing at all, you shall behold the Dearest Face.

ANGELUS SILESIUS

sauces,
salsas,
aromatics,
and
basics

BASIC SAUCES FOR HOT DISHES

BÉCHAMEL SAUCE
yield: 2 cups

> **2 Tbsps butter or margarine**
> **2 Tbsps cornstarch or all-purpose flour**
> **2 cups whole milk**
> **1 Tbsp dry sherry (optional)**
> **salt and pepper to taste**
> **pinch of freshly ground nutmeg (optional)**

Melt the butter in a good-sized stainless steel pan over medium-low heat. Add the cornstarch; stir continuously with a whisk. Add the milk, little by little, while whisking continuously. Add the sherry, salt, pepper, and nutmeg; continue stirring. When it begins to boil, reduce heat and continue cooking slowly until it thickens.

This sauce is excellent with fish and vegetables, and it is a necessary base for soufflés, omelettes, and other egg dishes,

MORNAY SAUCE
yield: 2 1/2 cups

> **2 cups Béchamel sauce (see recipe above)**
> **4 Tbsps grated Gruyère cheese**
> **4 Tbsps Romano or Parmesan cheese**
> **10 Tbsps heavy cream**

When the Béchamel sauce is at the boiling point, add the cheese and let it melt as the sauce thickens. When the sauce is ready, withdraw from the heat, and add the heavy cream while stirring continuously with a whisk or mixer.

> *Look to your heart*
> *that flutters in and out like a moth.*
> *God is not indifferent to your need.*
> *You have a thousand prayers but God has one.*
> ANNE SEXTON

WHITE SAUCE

yield: 1 1/2 cups

2 Tbsps cornstarch or all-purpose flour
1 1/2 cups milk
2 Tbsps butter or margarine
salt and freshly ground black pepper
dash of freshly ground nutmeg

Dissolve the cornstarch into a half cup of milk. Melt the butter in a medium-sized stainless steel pan over medium heat. When the butter begins foaming, add the milk and cornstarch and stir continuously. Add the rest of the milk, salt, pepper, and nutmeg; continue to stir until the sauce comes to a boil. Lower the heat and continue stirring until the sauce thickens. The sauce is ready when it is smooth and thick.

This sauce can be used as a basis for many other useful variations. It can be used on fish, meats, eggs, and vegetables.

WHITE SAUCE WITH MUSTARD

yield: 1 1/2 cups

Prepare the white sauce as described above. Add 1 teaspoon French or dry mustard. Stir until it has been mixed thoroughly.

WHITE SAUCE WITH HERBS

yield: 1 1/2 cups

Prepare the white sauce as described above. Add 3 tablespoons finely chopped and mixed herbs (tarragon, dill, parsley, thyme, and so on). Also add 1/2 teaspoon dry mustard and mix thoroughly.

WHITE SAUCE WITH WINE

yield: 1 3/4 cups

Prepare the basic white sauce as described above. Add 1/4 cup of white vermouth and 1/2 teaspoon dry mustard instead of nutmeg. Stir thoroughly until well mixed.

GREEN SAUCE
SAUCE VERTE

yield: 2 cups

Prepare a white sauce as directed above. Add 1/2 cup white wine and 1/2 cup finely chopped parsley. Mix thoroughly during the cooking process. This sauce can be used for a great variety of dishes.

HOLLANDAISE SAUCE

yield: 1 cup

1/2 cup butter, melted
3 egg yolks
juice of 1/4 lemon
1 Tbsp salt
1/4 tsp white pepper
1/3 cup boiling water
dash of nutmeg

Prepare the Hollandaise sauce by whisking the melted butter with a mixer and adding one egg yolk at a time while continuing to beat. Add the lemon juice, salt, pepper, nutmeg; continue whisking with the mixer. Just before serving, place the bowl in a saucepan with boiling water at the bottom. Over low heat, add to the sauce, little by little, the boiling water, stirring all the time until the sauce thickens. Remove the bowl from the saucepan before serving the sauce.

This sauce can be used on fish, veal, egg, and vegetable dishes.

TOMATO SAUCE

yield: 2 cups

6 Tbsps olive oil
1 large onion, finely chopped
3 garlic cloves, minced
2 lbs fresh tomatoes, peeled and sliced
3 Tbsps tomato purée
1 carrot, peeled and finely chopped
4 Tbsps fresh basil, finely chopped and minced
1 bay leaf
salt and fresh ground pepper to taste
pinch of dried thyme

Heat the olive oil in an enamel or stainless steel saucepan and slowly sauté the onion and garlic for a few minutes until they are soft and transparent. Add the remaining ingredients. Lower the heat and cook slowly for about 30 to 40 minutes, stirring from time to time. While the sauce is cooking, cover the saucepan partially, so that it remains moist and juicy. When the sauce is done, turn off the heat, cover the pan, and let it set for a few minutes before serving.

TOMATO SAUCE WITH WINE

Prepare the tomato sauce described above. Add 1 cup of red wine to the rest of the ingredients and cook slowly for about 40 to 45 minutes. This is a richer and smoother sauce. Both sauces can be used on pasta, fish, and egg dishes.

Every beauty seen here resembles more than anything else does,
that merciful fountain from which we all derive.
MICHELANGELO

MUSHROOM SAUCE
yield: 1 1/4 cups

1 oz butter or margarine
1 onion, finely chopped
1/2 pound fresh mushrooms, cut into small cubes
1 cup sherry or white wine
1/2 tsp ground turmeric
1/2 cup parsley, finely chopped
salt and freshly ground pepper to taste

Melt the butter in an enamel or stainless steel saucepan. Add the onion, mushrooms, sherry, turmeric, salt, and pepper; cook for a few minutes until the mushrooms begin to turn brown. Reduce the heat and add the parsley while stirring continuously. Cook thoroughly for another 4 to 5 minutes until the sauce is done.

This sauce is excellent on the top of rice, fish, meat, and eggs.

PESTO SAUCE
SAUCE AU PISTOU
yield: 1 cup

4 garlic cloves, minced
1 cup basil leaves, finely chopped
1/3 cup pistachio nuts, well chopped
1 cup olive oil (or more)
6 tsps grated Parmesan cheese
pinch of salt

Place the garlic and the basil in a mortar and mash with a pestle. Add the pistachio nuts and continue mashing them thoroughly. Place the mixture into a larger container, add the olive oil gradually, then the cheese and salt, and blend thoroughly.

A simpler and quicker way to prepare the pesto sauce is to place all the ingredients in a blender and mix thoroughly.

This is usually used with pasta, but it can also be used with gnocchi, seafood, eggs, and certain vegetables like zucchini.

ONION SAUCE
SAUCE AUX OIGNONS

yield: 2 cups

> **2 ozs butter**
> **4 medium onions, finely chopped**
> **1 cup dry white**
> **salt and pepper to taste**
> **1/2 cup heavy cream**

Melt the butter in a saucepan. Add the onions and sauté them over medium heat for a few minutes. Add the wine, salt, and pepper and cook slowly over low heat about 5 to 20 minutes, stirring from time to time. At the end, add the heavy cream and mix thoroughly.

This sauce can be used on eggs, potatoes, seafood, and certain meats.

RAVIGOTE SAUCE
SAUCE RAVIGOTE

yield: 1 cup

> **1 cup white sauce**
> **1/4 cup white wine**
> **1 Tbsp butter**
> **1/2 small onion, chopped**
> **1/4 tsp dry mustard**
> **1 tsp of each: parsley, tarragon, chervil (fresh or dried)**
> **salt and pepper to taste**

Prepare the white sauce as indicated on page 207. Heat the wine in a small saucepan. Sauté the onion in the butter, but do not allow it to brown. Add the hot wine and the white sauce. Stir continually. Add the mustard, herbs, salt, and pepper; blend all ingredients very well. Continue cooking and stirring the sauce for about two minutes, until the sauce becomes thick and creamy.

This delicious and easy to prepare sauce can be used with a variety of vegetables, with seafood, or over vegetable filled crêpes.

PARSLEY SAUCE
SAUCE AU PERSIL

yield: 2 cups

6 shallots, sliced and minced
3/4 cup white wine
1 bay leaf
1 cup vegetable stock
1 1/2 cup heavy cream
3/4 cup fresh parsley, minced
salt and pepper to taste

Pour the wine in a good-sized saucepan. Add the shallots and the bay leaf. Bring it to a boil while stirring constantly. Add the stock and continue stirring until it comes again to a boil. Lower the heat and continue boiling for 3 or 4 minutes, until the sauce is reduced to about 3/4 of a cup. At this point, add the cream, salt, and pepper. Blend and bring the sauce to another boil. Add the parsley, and continue cooking and stirring for another 5 to 6 minutes. Blend well the sauce and allow it to cool. When cool, pass the sauce through the blender. Pour the sauce back into the saucepan, and reheat it for one minute or two, stirring all the while. Serve hot.

This sauce can be used in a variety of ways, either over fish, vegetables, or egg dishes.

BASIC SAUCES FOR COLD DISHES

CREME CHANTILLY
yield: 1 cup

1 cup heavy cream
7 Tbsps confectioners' sugar
1 Tbsp vanilla extract
1 Tbsp French brandy

Pour the cream into a previously chilled bowl. Add the sugar, vanilla, and brandy. With a wire whisk, or yet the more practical electric beater, whip the cream until it becomes firm and thick. If need be, one may add more or lessen the amount of sugar in the cream according to one's taste. Chill it until ready to be used.

CRÈME FRAÎCHE
yield: 2 cups

1 cup heavy cream (not ultrapasteurized)
1 cup dairy sour cream

Whisk heavy cream and sour cream together in a bowl. Cover loosely with plastic wrap and let sit in kitchen, or other warm place overnight, or until thickened. Cover and refrigerate for at least 4 hours. The crème fraîche will then be thick and ready to use. It will last for up to 2 weeks in the refrigerator.

GARLIC SAUCE
SAUCE AOILI
yield: 1 cup

Prepare a mayonnaise sauce as indicated on page 215. Add 5 minced garlic cloves. Mix thoroughly and place the sauce in the refrigerator for several hours before using it.

This sauce can be used on seafood, salads, vegetables, and meats served cold.

TARRAGON SAUCE
SAUCE À L'ESTRAGON

yield: 1 cup

1/2 cup sour cream
3 Tbsps lemon juice
1/2 cup heavy cream
3 Tbsps chopped tarragon
salt and pepper to taste

Place all the above ingredients in a deep bowl and use a mixer to stir and blend thoroughly. Refrigerate until it is time to use. It can be used on salads and seafoods.

SIMPLE VINAIGRETTE
VINAIGRETTE CLASSIQUE

1 tsp salt
1/2 tsp freshly ground pepper
2 Tbsps wine vinegar
6 Tbsps olive oil

Place the salt and pepper in a cup or bowl. Add the vinegar and stir thoroughly. Add the oil and stir more until all the ingredients are completely blended.

VINAIGRETTE WITH MUSTARD
VINAIGRETTE À LA MOUTARDE

Prepare a simple vinaigrette as indicated above. Add 1 tablespoon French mustard and mix thoroughly.

VINAIGRETTE WITH GARLIC
VINAIGRETTE À L'AIL

Prepare a simple vinaigrette as indicated above. Add 1 crushed garlic clove. Let the vinaigrette stand for a few hours before using.

Vinaigrette With Herbs
VINAIGRETTE AUX HERBES

Prepare a simple vinaigrette as indicated on page 214, but replace the vinegar with the equivalent of lemon juice. Add 1/4 cup finely chopped herbs (parsley, tarragon, coriander, scallions, or so on). Mix thoroughly.

Sauce Mayonnaise
yield: 1 cup

1 egg yolk
2 tsps lemon juice (or tarragon vinegar)
1 tsp salt
1/2 tsp white pepper
1 tsp Dijon mustard
light olive oil or vegetable oil (about 3/4 cup)

Place the egg yolk in a bowl, add the mustard, salt, and pepper; mix with a whisk or a mixer. (It is simpler with a mixer.) Add the oil, little by little, while continuing to mix. In between, add the lemon juice and then resume adding the oil until the end when the mayonnaise thickens properly and is done. Keep the mayonnaise in the refrigerator until it is ready to be used.

The mayonnaise can be used in many ways, with hard-boiled eggs, potato salad, Russian salad, asparagus, and similarly.

Marinades and Salsas

Honey-Mustard Marinade

1/2 cup Dijon mustard
7 Tbsps honey
1/2 cup olive oil
1/3 cup fresh parsley, finely chopped, or dried
salt and freshly ground pepper to taste

Place all the above ingredients in a blender and mix well. This is an excellent marinade to use toward the end of the grilling process.

Sesame Oil and Soy Marinade

1/2 cup sesame oil
1/4 cup balsamic vinegar
3 Tbsps soy sauce
3 Tbsps dry onion flakes
5 Tbsps fresh cilantro, finally chopped
salt and pepper to taste

Place all the above ingredients in a deep bowl. Stir and mix very well by hand or with a mixer. Brush on oriental vegetables and others, fish chicken, and so on, prior to grilling.

HERB MARINADE

1/2 cup olive oil
1/3 cup balsamic vinegar
3 garlic cloves, finely minced
1 Tbsp dried thyme
1 Tbsp dried basil
1 Tbsp dried rosemary
1/2 Tbsp dried bay leaves, flaked
salt and pepper to taste

Place all the above ingredients in a deep bowl. Stir and mix well until ingredients are equally blended. Brush on vegetables, fish, and so on, at least 30 minutes before grilling.

ONION SALSA

1/2 cup peeled and chopped tomatoes
1 cup Vidalia onions, finely chopped
6 Tbsps olive oil
1/3 cup lime juice
3 garlic cloves, minced
1/4 cup fresh cilantro
1 jalapeño pepper, finely chopped
salt to taste

In a deep bowl, mix well all the above ingredients. Allow to stand several hours, so that flavors blend well before using as a marinade or condiment.

Aromatic or Flavored Oils and Vinegars

Herb-Scented Oil

3 cups olive oil
2 shallots, minced
2 bay leaves
1 sprig of rosemary
3 sprigs of thyme
1 sprig of basil

Pour the oil into the deep pot. Add the remaining ingredients and raise the heat to low-medium. Cook for 2 to 3 minutes. Turn the heat off and allow to cool.

When the oil cools, filter it through a fine colander into a very clean bottle. Keep it in a cool, dark place or refrigerate. Discard the other ingredients.

Spicy Oil

2 1/2 cups sesame oil
3 jalapeño peppers, minced
1 small onion, minced
3 garlic cloves, minced

Pour the oil into a deep casserole. Add the remaining ingredients. Raise the heat to low-medium for 2 to 3 minutes. Turn off the heat and allow it to cool.

When the oil cools, filter it through a fine colander into a very clean bottle. Keep it in a cool, dark place or refrigerate.

CITRUS-SCENTED OIL

2 1/2 cups olive oil
1 lemon peel, crushed
1 lime peel, crushed
1 orange peel, crushed
1/2 tsp lemon juice
a few peppercorns

Pour the oil into a deep pot. Add the remaining ingredients. Raise the heat to low-medium for 2 to 3 minutes. Stir well. Turn off the heat and allow it to cool.

When the oil cools, filter it through a fine colander into a very clear bottle. Keep it in a cool, dark place or refrigerate. Use for salads.

BASIL-SCENTED VINEGAR

3 cups red wine vinegar
3 garlic cloves, minced
1 cup fresh basil, finely chopped

Boil the vinegar in a deep casserole over medium heat for 3 to 4 minutes. Turn off the heat and add immediately the garlic and the basil. Cover the casserole and allow to cool for at least 2 hours or longer.

When the vinegar cools, filter it through a small fine colander into a very clean bottle. Keep it in a dark place or refrigerate. This vinegar is particularly good on a tomato salad. Be sure to discard the garlic and basil leaves.

LEMON VERBENA-SCENTED VINEGAR

3 cups cider vinegar
1 cup finely chopped lemon-verbena leaves
1 lemon peel, crushed

Boil the vinegar over medium heat for about 3 minutes. Turn off the heat and add the lemon-verbena leaves and the lemon peel. Cover the casserole and allow to cool.

Let the vinegar stand for at least 1 hour or longer, then filter it through a fine colander into a very clean bottle. Discard the remaining ingredients. Keep it in a dark, dry place or in the refrigerator. This vinegar is excellent on green salads and seafood salads.

SPICY BALSAMIC VINEGAR

3 cups balsamic vinegar
3 garlic cloves, minced
1 lemon peel, crushed
2 jalapeño peppers, minced

Pour the vinegar into a casserole and bring to a boil over medium heat. Add the garlic, lemon peel, peppers; reduce the heat to low-medium for 5 minutes. Turn off the heat and allow it to cool.

Let it stand for 1 hour or longer, then filter it through a fine colander into a very clean bottle. Discard the remaining ingredients. Keep it in a dark place or in the refrigerator. This vinegar is excellent on certain vegetables and salads.

Raspberry-Scented Vinegar

3 cups white wine vinegar
1 cup fresh raspberries
1 Tbsp rum

Boil the vinegar over medium heat for about 3 minutes. Add the raspberries, the rum, and lower the heat to low and continue cooking for about 2 minutes. Turn off the heat. With the help of a masher, crush the raspberries, cover the casserole, and allow the vinegar to cool.

When the vinegar has cooled, pour the entire thing (with the fruit) into a clean sterilized glass container. A large canning jar is perfect for this. Place it in the refrigerator for 1 week. After 1 week, filter the mixture through a colander into a clean bottle, discarding the fruit. Keep the bottle in a dark place or refrigerate. This is a superb vinegar for green salads.

PASTRY

FINE DOUGH FOR TARTS AND QUICHES
LA PÂTÉ BRISÉE

1 egg
1 cup flour
1 stick of butter or margarine
5 Tbsps ice water
pinch of salt

Prepare the pastry shell by mixing all the ingredients in a good-sized bowl. Use both a fork and your hands for mixing. Do not overwork the dough. Form a ball with the dough and sprinkle with flour. Place the dough in the refrigerator for at least 1 hour and let it rest. When the dough is ready to be worked, sprinkle some flour over the table or a board and carefully roll out the dough, extending it in every direction. Butter a tart or pie dish thoroughly and place the rolled dough into it with care. The dough must always be handled with the fingers. Trim the edges in a decorative fashion. Cover the pastry shell with aluminum foil and place in the oven at 250° to 300° F for about 12 to 15 minutes for prebaking period.

This recipe is basically used for salty dishes: quiches, vegetable or meat tarts.

SWEET FINE DOUGH FOR FRUIT TARTS AND PIES
LA PÂTÉ BRISÉE SUCRÉE

Prepare the basic dough recipe given above but substitute 1 stick of sweet butter and do not add salt. One may also add an extra egg for a richer pie crust.

This recipe can be used for dessert dishes, fruit tarts, and pies.

RICH PASTRY DOUGH
(FOR A CRUNCHY DESSERT)

1 egg
1 cup whole wheat flour
1 tsp baking powder
8 ozs sweet butter or margarine
1 tsp brown sugar
1 Tbsp vegetable oil
2 Tbsps pecan nuts, finely chopped
8 Tbsps ice water (more if needed)
pinch of salt

Prepare the pastry shell by mixing all the ingredients and following the instructions given above for fine dough for tarts and quiches. The combination of the whole wheat flour and the nuts provide a splendid and richer texture to the crust and gives a nuttier flavor to tarts and pies.

This crust is excellent for open tarts and pies.

O Thou who clothest the lilies of the field
and feedest the birds of the air,
Who leadest the sheep to pasture
and the hart to the water's side,
Who has multiplied loaves and fishes
and converted water to wine.
Do thou come to our table
as Giver and Guest to dine.
BLESSING OF FOOD AND WINE

SODIUM-FREE HERBS AND SPICE BLENDS

These seasoning mixes are made with dried herbs and spices. If you wish to use herbs from your garden, dry them by hanging in bunches in an airy clean space, out of the sun. When crisp to the touch, crumble the herbs with your fingers, discarding the stems. Measure the ingredients for an herb blend into a bowl and rub together with fingers to mix. Store in airtight containers out of the light.

BOUQUET PROVENÇAL
(FOR VEGETABLES, SAUCES, MEATS)

1 tsp thyme
1 tsp basil
1/2 tsp rosemary
1/2 tsp sage
bay leaf (use whole, remove before serving food)

BLESSING OF HERBS

You have made heaven and earth, and all things visible and invisible,
and have enriched the earth with plants and trees
for the use of men and animals.
You appointed each species to bring forth fruit of its own kind,
not only to serve as food for living creatures,
but also as medicine for sick bodies.
With mind and body, we earnestly implore you, in your goodness,
to bless those various herbs and add to
their natural powers the healing power of your grace.
May they keep off disease and adversity from
the men and beasts who use them in our name.

AN OLD RUSSIAN PRAYER

Prunelle de Mes Yeux
(FOR VEGETABLES, MEAT, GRAINS)

1 tsp dry mustard
1/2 tsp sage
1/2 tsp thyme
1/2 tsp white pepper
1 tsp chives

Mes Épices
(FOR VEGETABLES, SEAFOOD, SAUCES)

3/4 tsp parsley flakes
1/2 tsp onion powder
1 tsp sweet red pepper
1 tsp tarragon
1/4 tsp paprika
1/2 tsp lemon flakes

Herbes Melangées
(FOR VEGETABLES, SAUCES, POULTRY)

1/2 tsp garlic powder
1/2 tsp marjoram
1/2 tsp thyme
1/2 tsp oregano
1/2 tsp sage
1/2 tsp chives

index